Balboa Press books may be ordered through booksellers or by contacting:

Balboa Press
A Division of Hay House
1663 Liberty Drive
Bloomington, IN 47403
www.balboapress.com.au
1 (877) 407-4847

Print information available on the last page.

ISBN: 978-1-5043-0311-8 (sc)
ISBN: 978-1-5043-0312-5 (e)

Balboa Press rev. date: 07/06/2016

For Jams and Pickles

The Story of Owen and Kaye Pope and the growth of their Anathoth brand of Jams and Pickles, as told by Kaye Pope.

Owen Pope Introduces Pope's Passion

We all have our own values, principles, or standards that guide the way we live our lives and the decisions we make. It is not easy to determine what our values and priorities are. We can speak out our values, but our actions and behaviours can contradict our spoken values when we do not act them out. For example, if I say, 'I love swimming in the sea,' someone asks when I last swam in the sea, and I reply a couple of years ago, that is proof that swimming in the sea is not a high value. Market research is often misleading because it is verbal, and people reveal the truth not by what they say but in their actions. They can say they love Anathoth Jam, but if they don't buy any, what does that tell us?

When a value-driven lifestyle is identified, strived for, and revealed through action, it is a fulfilled life and is imprinted on everything we do. It becomes the essence by which we live. It offers protection against other people's behaviours, by not allowing their behaviours to govern our own behaviour.

Have you identified your values?

I have already identified my values, and they govern my business practices and my behaviour. It was my goal and the values I adopted that helped me to establish and build the Anathoth business. I would not have succeeded as I did if this were not so.

I endeavour to display my values by putting them at the core of business relationships. Today we live and conduct business in an environment that promotes the market, where the price for goods and services are not necessarily their worth but is related to the wealth of the consumer. The market greed that is prevalent in today's business is all about screwing down vulnerable suppliers! But quality products and reasonable profits can still be made while ensuring everyone supplying the business gets a reasonable slice of the pie, to enable people to earn a living and stay supplying.

As our business grew, my focus was not on protecting my wealth. I focused on generating work and income and starting new businesses. Decisions I made in establishing and growing my business would have been different had I been governed by the will to protect my wealth, and the growth in our business would not have been achieved. If business growth is what a country is looking for, then the law must protect the entrepreneurs' wealth, because if it's left to those who spend their energy and focus on protecting their wealth, the two goals are not compatible.

I am always thinking about where I am going, and I encourage others to move beyond what they might normally accept, speak the truth, deal honestly, and live uprightly.

However, how did the real story start? With a stall in the world-famous Nelson Market.

Along with my dear wife, who chose to write down our story, my thanks go to all those involved in the success of building the Anathoth brand from 1987 until 2004. They were years of life-changing experiences for all involved, our family members, and our many customers who went out and sold the jam for us, the media, who celebrated with us, the business associates who supported us and the supermarkets, who gave us the opportunity for success. We treasure the wonderful memories we made together as we journeyed through the years developing the Anathoth Brand.

Owen Pope
Queensland, Australia
2016

Contents

Part 1

Part 2

Part 3

Part 4

Part 5

PART 1

Youthful Choices

Owen as a small boy

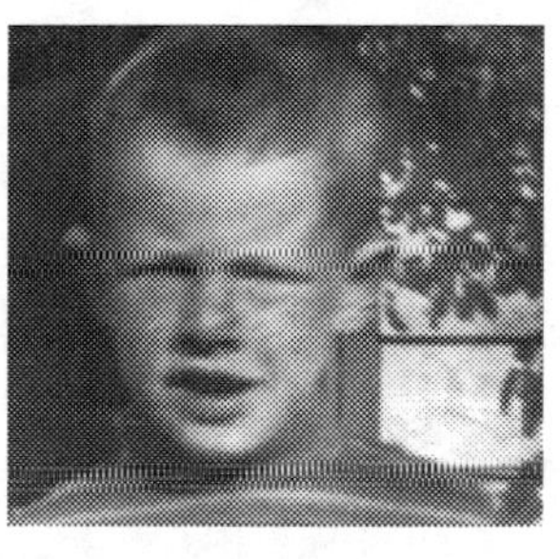

In the small New Zealand farming community of Haldane, situated at the far end of the South Island, the Macrocarpa trees grow horizontally because of the strong, salt-laden, westerly winds. It was in this place that Owen Pope was born and raised. In this rural community, farming was often the topic of conversation, and it wasn't unusual for the young to be asked, 'What kind of a farmer are you going to be?'

The expected response was to voice an aspiration to be either a sheep or dairy farmer, but because the young fellow in question was drinking raspberry cordial and enjoying it so much, he looked at the bottle reflectively and replied, 'I want to be a raspberry farmer.'

As it turned out, this would be a self-fulfilling prophecy. The life of a raspberry farmer was to become one of the many challenges Owen embarked upon in later life.

Southland Boy's High School was where the farmers of the district sent their sons, and Owen was no exception to that tradition. He valued the four years spent living with his colleagues in the Coldstream Hostel, and he had some personal success in the academic field. He is still able to recollect the big day that Lance Blakie, the geography and bookkeeping teacher in his upper-fifth class, handed out the results of the bookkeeping exam. Owen recounted, 'I watched Mr. Blakie as he strolled around the class handing out the papers. I saw him pull out one sheet and put it on the bottom of the pile. I asked myself, 'What's he up to?' It wasn't long before I found out. After handing all the other boys their papers, Mr. Blakie held up the last paper, looked over the top of his spectacles (as he always did), and handed me my test paper. As he did so, he uttered words that stayed with me for life: 'You're a funny fellow, Pope. I don't understand you – bottom in geography and top in bookkeeping!'

'I was elated. I saw my results as a major achievement. After failing my last exam, I had decided to spend more time studying the subject I found the easiest, bookkeeping. Making that decision resulted in my doubling my marks.'

As many young farmers' sons did at that time, Owen returned home to work on the family farm after four years of secondary school. There he awaited his school certificate results.

The school certificate was a much-sought-after academic achievement at this time. Students had to achieve an average score of at least a C grade (50–64 per cent) or better in at least five subjects, including English and mathematics. Owen remembered his father being unusually eager to walk down to the roadside rural mailbox that day, obviously aware that the results were due. His face lit up with glee as he handed over the letter. The memory still fresh in his mind, Owen recalled how he yelled in great excitement, 'I passed! I passed!' at the top of his lungs. This was a momentous milestone, one of which he and his father were most certainly proud.

This academic success did not inspire him to return to school. He was a young fella whose only ambition was to own a set of wheels, and sooner rather than later! But after only a few months working on the family farm, when the isolation of country life became too much for his gregarious nature to bear, he left the farm and headed to the city of Invercargill, where he dreamed of learning to fly and becoming a top-dressing pilot.

Unfortunately, his father, aware that the danger of flying near to the ground frequently led to many crashes in those early days, was upset with his youngest son's latest career choice. As such, he offered no support. Owen was only eighteen at the time and was sensitive to his father's wishes, so he went looking for other opportunities.

He was accepted for teacher's training college, but the eight-pounds-a-week pay was a big deterrent (especially when another potential employer, the ANZ Bank, offered eleven pounds).

Owen as a young man

Occupational Switching

Once Owen started working at the bank, it wasn't long before he achieved his goal of owning a set of wheels, and he became the proud owner of a second-hand Vauxhall car. However, over time with his rented flat becoming a venue for after-work parties, he found himself trapped in a very flamboyant lifestyle that cost too much. His solution? Find an even better-paying job.

At that time, people in their twenties jumping between jobs were seen as both wayward and noncommittal. Owen ignored conventional wisdom in this area. He decided that if it improved his chances of finding more satisfying and higher-paying employment, he would tolerate the stigma entirely. Desperate to increase his income yet again, he left the bank and took a job wool pressing for an agricultural firm called Wrightsons, where he expected to earn twenty-eight thirty-five pounds per week! It was a physically demanding and repetitive job: lining the wool press with a large synthetic bag resembling sackcloth, filling it with rolled fleeces, compressing it down with a powerful mechanical ram, and sewing up the end of the bale.

While Owen was working at Wrightsons, the synthetic fibres began to be used for carpet manufacturing. When

Britain joined the European Economic Community, export markets were restricted, causing wool prices to plummet. Owen kept busy storing wool in sheds and halls around the province. Farmers had it rough until the wool was sold years later, when demand returned and prices on the world market improved.

Contract work suited Owen. He loved the competitive spirit he found amongst the team of workers. Their average output was thirty bales an hour, but not satisfied with that, they worked harder and set themselves new records: forty-five to forty-eight bales an hour. The seasonal nature of the wool-pressing industry (November to April) enabled Owen to work through the winter back on the farm at Haldane, or to tour around New Zealand with his mates.

After three years of wool pressing, Owen decided to change occupations yet again, but things were different this time. When he returned home to work on the farm, he was married. He decided to supplement his income by working in a bar, at the only drinking establishment in Southern Southland, the Tokanui Tavern. When a new tavern was built at Woodlands, the opportunity for full-time employment as a barman came up. He found this job very satisfying, and he worked with the directors to set up facilities and entertainment for the new tavern.

A few years later, with the tavern sold, the new owners offered Owen the lease. Now he had a family to support, so after deciding that there were too many maybes in the deal, he grabbed the opportunity to join a start-up team as a metal coordinator in the new aluminium smelter at Tiwai Point, where the pay was good.

Fallout from a Broken Marriage

Owen did well financially while working at the smelter. After he realised his long-awaited dream of learning to fly, he made many cross-country trips with the Invercargill Aero Club.

After six years at Tiwai, when big money was earned (and spent), Owen endured a few months of suspicion that his wife was having an affair. Tormented by not knowing the truth, he hired someone to investigate his wife's activities. When he left his job, his wife left him, taking the children and their furniture with her. The motivation to carry on making money to provide for dependants vanished. The financial ground he'd gained was lost. Owen felt that part of him had been destroyed, never to be repaired or replaced.

He had known the heavy weight of responsibility he was committing to when he married at the age of twenty-three. He had embarked on the long-standing and very strong family tradition of placing the needs of family before his own. These were values he held dear to his heart (and he still does today), but they were not the same ideals as his wife's. The practices and lifestyles they each chose were not compatible, and separation and divorce were inevitable. He came to regret the fact that he had ignored his friends and family, who'd advised him that the match wouldn't work because of these differences. He continually repremanded himself for not heeding their warnings. Owen had three children from his first marriage, and when conflict arose over access, he fought a long, hard battle with the legal system through the high court to reestablish contact.

Although Owen won the case, it was a matter of winning the battle but not the war for access. Owen was left in a powerless position with grief and the loss as his daily companions.

The pain of being pushed around – as well as having his relationship with his children withdrawn on a whim – was exacerbated by the complications of working within a cumbersome legal system. It was more than he could bear. He didn't want to play the game with the rules changing all the time. In order to put an end to the game, he quit his efforts. He then divorced his wife and never saw his children again for eleven years. For Owen, this was worse than knowing his children were dead; grieving was not an option when he knew they were still alive, just unreachable!

While in recovery from the broken relationship and loss of access to his three young children, Owen joined a team to sell insurance. He was good at selling and had previously attended a course years before on selling encyclopaedias. During his two-day course, a world of information was pumped into him, and it was so intense he came out unable to remember where the car was parked.

When selling insurance did nothing to improve his outlook on life, he found a job working at Allied Concrete as a batch operator, making up the concrete for the truck loads going out.

Together at Last

I was teaching at South School Invercargill when Owen and I first met at a local dance. Like Owen, I had suffered from a broken relationship.

But unlike Owen, who had spent all of his life in Southland, from the time I was born I had never spent longer than four years in one place. My father, a policeman, was continually transferred throughout my childhood from one town to another. We went from Dunedin to Kaniere, Green Island, Greymouth, Kawera, Reefton, and Westport. I never chose where I lived, and neither did I choose the subjects I would take at secondary school. My father decided a commercial course was the best option for future employment.

I completed my secondary years at Greymouth High School and left with a university entrance qualification. The day I left school, my dad found me employment as a shorthand typist in the office of the Grey Hospital Board. It wasn't long before my boss, Kevin O'Leary, discovered that I could take down shorthand during dictation, but I failed when it came to translating it back accurately. My heart was not in it, so after a spell on the hospital telephone exchange, I decided to fulfill my life time ambition of working with children and applied for training college. Being accepted for Christchurch Training College meant that for the first time, I moved before my parents, but it wasn't long before they were on the move again. This time it was to Kawerau, a paper mill town in the North Island.

During my summer break, my dad got me a job in the office at the Kawerau paper mill. A year later, another transfer took my parents to Reefton, on the West Coast of the South Island. My first teaching position at Cobden School was less than an hour's drive away.

After a years teaching in Cobden, I moved to the bright lights of Wellington City in search of adventure. I was unable to find a teaching position immediately, so I found employment with a solicitor, as his wife's companion until a teaching job came up at the newly built Cannon Creek School, a short train ride from Wellington. I only stayed for one term because I succeeded in getting the teaching position I really wanted, in Suva, Fiji.

After two wonderfully exciting years living the high life in Suva with twelve other single New Zealand teachers, I moved to Sydney, Australia. I taught in the outer suburb of Woollongon for six months before returning to Wellington for a spell at Clyde Quay School.

I flatted in Wellington with a girlfriend I had known and taught with in Suva. I was a bridesmaid at her wedding, and I met and later married her younger brother. Because he was in the army at Waioru, we set up home in Taihape, where I taught at the local primary school until the children were born. Then an opportunity for employment with family found us moving to Invercargill. After suffering nine years of a difficult marriage, losing our second son at three months old in a cot death, and physical abuse from an unemployed husband, I left our family home with two small children and found myself back in the workforce. First I worked as a shipping clerk at the Tiwai Smelter, and then I taught at South School Invercargill.

I had been separated from my husband for over a year, bought a house, and created a new life for myself. Then I met Owen at a local dance in Gore. I was ready for a new relationship. He drank whiskey and had lovely red hair like my father, so when he asked me to marry him just seven days after we met, how could I turn him down? We continued our whirlwind romance for some time and then married. I sold my house, and we purchased a larger house together in South Invercargill.

After our marriage, he legally adopted my children as his own, and it aroused in Owen the ambition and desire to advance his employment. He accepted a job with the Ministry of Works as a stores clerk for custody control and purchasing. Later he was transferred to the accounting section and was trained as a cost clerk for the electrical, mechanical, and carpentry workshops.

His boss reported that Owen approached his work methodically and systematically, showed sound judgement, and maintained good relationships with people. With such a positive report, another promotion looked to be on the horizon.

Nelson on the Agenda

It was a cold November day in Invercargill. Owen and I sat watching the hail mounting up on the windowsill, with the gas fire burning and the pot-bellied stove blazing away, so it was no surprise when in exasperation he declared, 'There must be somewhere better to live than this. It's either the Bay of Islands or Nelson. Let's start applying for jobs.'

I opted for Nelson because it was close to Westport, where my parents lived. Besides, I was a mainlander at heart.

Nelson is called the sunshine capital of New Zealand, and like many people who enjoyed blue skys and warm days, we had made it our favourite holiday spot. Its farming and forestry economy would give us not only more sunshine but the country lifestyle we enjoyed. The move to greener pasturers was a chance to leave past hurts behind and start afresh as a family, building a new life together.

Owen's employment with the Ministry of Works gave him the opportunity to apply for an all-expenses-paid transfer and promotion. Once a decision to move had been made, Owen acted quickly, and by January 1981 he had won two positions in Nelson, one with the Forest Service and the other with the Department of Labour. After reading the job descriptions, he decided on the Forest Service because it was a new position involving setting up procedures, a challenge he found statisfying. Owen left almost immediately to take up his appointment, and I stayed with the children until our house was sold three months later.

Finding a house to purchase in Nelson at this time proved difficult because there were few on the market, but on a visit to the aeroclub, Owen mentioned to someone that he was looking for a house to buy. Fortunately for us, wheels within wheels were working, and the following day Owen had a call from a land agent, who told him of a house that was about to come onto the market. Bob Stanton, the owner, was willing to sell, and a deal was made, much to Owen's relief. He drew a plan of the house and posted it to me. I found myself trusting his judgement and agreeing to buy. We had a deposit from our house sale for the first mortgage, but we needed to raise a second mortgage to cover the purchase price.

I gained a senior teaching position at Wakefield School, and our daughter, Shelley, travelled the twenty minutes from Richmond with me. Our son, Timothy, was enrolled in Waimea Intermediate, where for the first time his name was shortened to Tim.

The first year in Richmond was spent renovating our newly purchased, three-bedroom 1950s bungalow. We started within about two weeks of moving in. My parents had arrived to stay with us, and Owen decided to chainsaw out an opening in the outside wall off the kitchen, in order to put in a ranchslider.

Both my and Owen's parents loved being involved in our projects. The alteration went according to plan, and over the next few years, we continued to renovate the property until it was finally completed to our satisfaction.

Unfortunately, nine months after Owen was appointed to the Forest Service, a woman appealed the appointment on the grounds of discrimination. Although she was not qualified or experienced for the position, there had been a statement made during her interview that because the job involved visits to the forestry camps, where only men lived, the employer wanted a man. There have been very good historical reasons for these decisions, but she won the appeal and was appointed to the position on the grounds of discrimination – only to last six months in the job.

Unemployment was not on our agenda when we'd made our financial commitments. We were devastated when Owen was made redundent. It was a double blow for Owen because he was enjoying setting up the new procedures for this position. With hat in hand, he visited the Department of Labour. Luck was on his side because the job he had previously applied for as an employment officer came up again. With his paperwork still on file, he was able to be appointed and commence work immediately.

When he took up the position, his new boss, Guy Romano, reprimanded him for not having taken the position the first time round, and he added, 'You would have had a promotion by now!'

The Fun Years

Life had become very comfortable, and we settled into the welcomed change after our traumatic earlier years. We loved the frequent visits from family members, especially our parents; Owen parents came from Invercargill, and mine came from Westport. Then we were thrilled when, after two years of holiday visits, Owen's parents expressed a desire to buy a house in Richmond. Owen found them a new town house built on Wensley Road. Owen's mum decided she liked it very much, and after they determined that the move would be beneficial, Owen facilitated it. He helped them choose the colours to complete the interior of the house, picked new furniture, and enjoyed landscaping the section before they moved in.

After the move, it was holiday time with Owen's parents, along with weekend drives exploring the district. It was so good to have family around. We took the opportunity to join the world-famous Pelorus Mail Run with the Glenmore Cruises, where we visited isolated homesteads nestled in quiet, secluded bays,

Owen on a school camp.

delivering supplies and mail. We visited Collingwood and Pupu Springs, and Owen went on at least two school camps per year. We took day outings to the waterfall in the Aniseed Valley, went to the swimming hole in the Lee Valley, and had a climb up the Richmond Hill to the forestry lookout, which was not the cultivated track that exists today!

Saturdays were busy with athletic meetings, tennis matches, and some evenings with committee meetings for the Waimea School Parent Teacher Association.

Owen joined Weight Watchers, and I went along as a support person to learn about his food requirements. I took some control by weighing up his servings. He was good at setting goals and achieving them, and so within a year he reached his goal weight and became a lifetime member. However, after maintaining his weight for some time, he gradually put it back on. His excuse was that one day I said I had had enough of weighing up his food, and he agreed, so the previous arrangement went out the window.

I fondly remember the memory of Christmas 1983. It was the year Owen bought Timothy a computer for Christmas – a Sinclair ZX81, one of the very earliest models. The competition between them to see who could learn about that computer first was something else! It was worse than the fight over leftover mashed potatoes. Owen, who loved new gadgets, would stay up half the night trying to figure out how it worked and how much more he could learn on it. Then Timothy would be up and at it the next day. This passion did not subside until they had exhausted all they could do with this computer – which compared with today's computers was probably not much!

Everything was going well financially. There were many social activities and family events, and we had lots of support and participation in our lives from our parents and other family members who enjoyed holidaying in Nelson. Owen and I were on good salaries, and there was money for a new car and other projects.

Building a New House

After a few years of hard saving and getting on our feet financially, Owen decided that the garage on our property, with a room at the back and an entrance onto a back street, could be made into a holiday place for the many family members who came to visit. He consulted the local council with his idea, and to his delight he discovered that it was possible to build a new three-bedroom house on the back of the section. He became excited and could not stop talking about the opportunity. The motivation he began with, to house extended family, was quickly overtaken by his new vision: a brand-new house for us.

'Why make do with a makeshift building when a new house can be built? The houses we have lived in and altered cost us a fair bit of money, and at the end of the day, you still have an old house!' he reasoned with me.

After much consultation with folks in the know, Owen decided that building a new house on the back of our section was a real possibility. A big project, but a doable one!

He fervently researched the number of working hours involved in building this house. Then he calculated the period the project would take, and he estimated that the house would take one thousand man-hours to complete.

If we both worked every night for two hours, and every weekend, we could complete the house in twelve months. After deciding that we were up to the challenge, it was game on!

The first step was designing the layout of the house, and we spent many hours deliberating and planning its design, trying to achieve the flow appropriate for our lifestyle. However, when working on the plan by ourselves became stressful and unproductive, Owen decided to invest in the best architect in town, Ian Jack.

We presented ourselves to his receptionist on the day of our appointment, and when Ian Jack discovered that our booking was not there, he offered us a quick ten minutes at no charge. We were very lucky because it turned out to be the most valuable ten minutes we'd ever spent. On seeing our rough plan, he quickly showed us how, by moving the kitchen from the east wall to the west, we could achieve the desired flow of living that we wanted. He also gave us a vision for the rest of the house, which had now become two stories. With the plans drawn up in detail Owen could not to be deterred or discouraged from reaching the goal.

Owen had always been very good at getting people's cooperation and gleaning information. He would research thoroughly and would not proceed until he had gathered and understood all the relevant information that stood him in good stead for this mammoth project. He created the house in every detail in his mind before hammering in the first nail.

At the time we were ready to put down the foundations, my nephew, John Purcell, a builder, was staying with us to attend Polytechnic. He put down the concrete foundations for the new house. Owen hired two builders for three days to erect the pre-cut frame. Then Owen, who hates heights, and I hauled and nailed onto the roof many sheets of iron until it was covered. The gib-board went on next, and Owen's sister Rosalie and her husband, Steve (a builder), were home from Sydney for their parents' fiftieth wedding anniversary. When the angles on the scotia presented a problem, Steve and Owen's brother, Frank, pitched in. When my nephew Patrick came to do an electrical course at Polytechnic, he stayed with us and did the electrical wiring on the house, which was checked out by a registered electrician.

The day the pre-cut stairs went in place was an event to remember. Many family members gathered to give Owen helpful suggestions about how the ready-made angled stairs would actually fit into the already prepared stairwell. The discussions and suggestions and the moving of these stairs into different positions and angles took a couple of hours, and still the stairs could not be put in place.

Finally, hunger pangs took over, and the crowd disappeared into our house for a meal. A short time later, Owen came in with a beaming smile on his face and announced, 'It's done!'

'We don't believe it,' the chorus echoed from everyone seated around the dinner table, and they rushed out to see.

This man was truly amazing. The task was completed, and the stairs were in place and looked great.

Owen and I had immersed ourselves in the building project and had spent every weekend and evening focused on the project to complete it in twelve months, as Owen had calculated. We rented out our old home and moved into the brand-new home full of wonderful memories left by all the family members who had helped us complete this ambitious task. Owen was proud of his effort and enjoyed the new home so much that I never thought he would ever leave it, but he decided that it was exciting to be around happening things and see plans come together, so I was left wondering what he would get up to next!

Not long after we had moved into the new house, Owen's dad, who had worked hard on the building project, became so sick that he needed to be hospitalized. He passed away a couple of years later.

We lived in the house for three years and then decided it was time to challenge ourselves on a new project. But I am getting ahead of myself here, because there were many events that led up to that next life-changing project!

You Are Free Indeed

In June 1984, Owen heard Bob Jones, leader of the newly formed New Zealand Party, speak about freedom and prosperity. The prime minister of New Zealand, Robert Muldoon, was a strong believer in the need for state intervention and control of the economy, but Bob Jones had no liking for these policies, and Jones's newly formed New Zealand Party soon developed a sizable following of likeminded people. Owen was captivated by the message and joined the campaign trail with other Richmond businessmen. We went to the inaugural conference in Wellington and had our first political experience. Enough National Party voters chose to vote for this new political party, and although it won no seats, the vote splitting enabled the Labour Party to win the 1984 election. Robert Muldoon was gone!

After this foray into politics, it was time to move on. Owen became aware of an opportunity to grow turf for the new property developments that were happening around the Nelson area. While landscaping our house and his parents' property, Owen had developed a passion for plants. When the opportunity came to grow turf and establish a plant nursery in Richmond, it appealed to him. Each day on the way to work, he drove past the few undeveloped acres on Salisbury Road, which he viewed as a perfect area for growing turf and running a nursery.

His idea for the nursery was smouldering when he met nurseryman Ross Baldwin, who came into the Department of Labour (where Owen worked) looking for staff. Owen shared his vision with Ross, who was very enthusiastic about the idea of a nursery on Salisbury Road because he was about to move his nursery from Tahunanui. Ross suggested that they work together on the project. Owen agreed and approached the landowner, who agreed to sell them the land. Owen then did extensive investigation and research, spending many hours evaluating and analyzing the potential of the proposed project. With council approval, the plan moved ahead. Because the site already had existing trees on it, they called the nursery Arbor-Lea.

After investigating the proposal and giving it serious consideration, Owen realized that much financing would be needed to get the nursery off the ground. He decided to pull out because it did not look like a watertight investment for us at this time. Ross then went on to find others to invest, and he built a nursery and turf business. Years later he sold the block as a housing development, which retained the name Arbor-Lea.

This same year we received a visit from the local Anglican minister, Jim Dyer, asking if we could help lead a youth group. Owen and I had both had training in Invercargill with the Human Relationship Centre, so we felt equipped to assist with the group and agreed to share the leadership with Pam Powers, a former missionary who had the scriptural knowledge to keep us on track.

After a few months of involvement with the youth group, a team from Church Army, an evangelistic ministry within the Anglican Church, arrived to do a couple of weeks' ministry. Their team leader was Wendy Woods, who travelled around in her gypsy caravan. Soon after arriving, Wendy and her team organized a gathering for the youth and their leaders. The meeting started with a few introductory games and then broke off into groups for a discussion on the question 'Is there more than one way to God?'

Owen's thoughts raced rampantly through his head at a mile a minute, and they went something like this: 'All religions are basically the same. Even though Christianity might be different, it's just one philosophy among many, and it's only as valid as any other religion. Even if there are differences between religions, they all have equal claims on the truth. You have your truth, and I have my truth. We ought to be loving and respectful and accepting toward people of all faiths, such as Buddhism and Hinduism.'

A senior college student, Kevin South, whose voice rang with confidence and conviction, interrupted these thoughts and shattered Owen's theories to pieces. 'Jesus said, "I am the way and the truth and the life. No one comes to the Father except through me." It's John 14:6.'

Owen hastily slammed shut his open mouth, which had been ready to let out some of his internalized dialogue. This claim the Bible makes can rankle people like nothing else! Kevin's quote caused Owen to have a eureka moment in which his understanding and experience came together, and he heard the truth of the Christian message – as he tells everyone, his moment of conversion.

Knowing the truth sets, you free!

From then on, Owen became an enthusiastic new Christian, hungry and wanting to be fed. When he heard about a summer school Christian Advance Ministries was holding in Palmerston North, he was quick to use it as a venue for a family holiday.

The main speaker at the conference was Colin Urquhart, an Anglican minister from England. The teachings throughout the week were of great benefit and covered many topics. However, it was during the Sunday morning service, when Colin began ministering to the congregation, that Owen received the greatest gift. 'There is someone here, who has received enormous damage and hurt from a person he had relationship with. God wants to work through him, but he needs to forgive this person for the pain she has caused him.'

Owen stood up with a great sob. I squirmed in my seat, as a group of people descended upon him, praying as he relived the painful experiences of the past, until he was able to offer and acknowledge the forgiveness necessary for the healing of the emotional pain he had been carrying for years. Only then did his tears subside.

As Owen received ongoing ministry, and as he studied and gained some understanding of the Bible, he began to feel the freedom he desired. He described it as if he had been in a dark cave and was now coming out into the light of day. 'When I stood outside of Christianity, I was supposedly unlimited by its rules and restrictions, but after entering the room labelled Christianity, I discovered that I had already been in a room, and now I was outside, where there was complete freedom of choice.'

Not long after Owen's conversion, John Wimber, the leader of the Vineyard Movement in America, came to town. Wimber's teachings had a major impact on Owen's life!

A Man Called Wimber, 1934–1997

The Vineyard Movement originated in California in 1974 and attracted a wide range of people with a desire to experience and share their faith in God. John Wimber had a major influence on the church as a hymn writer, lecturer, author, pastor, evangelist, church growth consultant, and builder of the Vineyard Movement, which is a neo-charismatic Evangelical Christian denomination that began in the United States and spread to many countries worldwide.

Owen's first contact with Vineyard was when John Wimber held the Signs, Wonders and Church Growth Conference in Auckland in 1986. Owen connected and felt right at home with the core values of Vineyard. Their values and priorities gripped Owen's heart and influenced his life dramatically over the next few years as he attended many conferences. Owen began buying Wimber's easy to understand teaching and church-planting tapes, and he listened to over six hundred hours of them. They were messages from the Bible and gave a clear understanding of human nature demonstrated by his actions.

'Jesus knew that if he did what he did, then he would end up the way he did.'

Jesus Christ became Owen's passion in life.

The Bible says, 'The heart of man reflects man' (Prov. 27:19).

When you understand what drives your behaviour, you will also understand your heart. When you understand your heart better, you will understand something vital: being able to cooperate with God and help yourself grow spiritually.

John Wimber's words resonated with Owen, and his teachings became understandings and practices. Owen came to understand that people join the church for different reasons, but they only stay for one, and that is relationship! He taught his congregations to love the whole church because, as he said, 'Vineyard is only one vegetable in the stew.'

He taught that programmes were only workable as long as they work; when they quit working, we should quit working them! He called for people to love the unlovable, which is easy to do when sitting at home watching television. If you don't even like people but you can go out and love them, that's where the rubber meets the road!

We live in an age of self-pursuit, he would say, and genuine, warm hospitality is a practical example of unselfish giving.

When people experience God's love, they invariably say, 'Give me some of that.' Is it any wonder that after the first conference, Owen left with a thirst for more? He attended all the Vineyard conferences in New Zealand, and he listened to teaching tapes and worship music. He profoundly changed his perception over the next few years and had a desire to visit Anaheim Vineyard.

Faith Generates Security

Owen says, 'When experienced as reality, faith generates a feeling of deep security. Having a high level of assurance that my expectations will be fulfilled reduces the need to avoid risk and leads to a maturity enabling me to embrace intimacy and trust.'

He began enthusiastically taking part in church life at Holy Trinity Richmond, organizing youth camps, rallies, house meetings, guitar lessons, and many other enjoyable social gatherings. He soon became churchwarden.

Then the young people brought their band, including drums, into the service and caused a great deal of heartache for those people who had difficulty embracing the changes. With the new technology of the 1980s, the overhead projector introduced into the church, Owen was able to overcome opposition from congregation members by communicating openly about his plan. He tastefully attached the screen to the beam of the church and hid it in a specially built pelmet, so that it did not detract from the beauty of the beams. He also built a stand for the projector that blended in with the existing decor. My, how technology has changed in a few decades, and Owen always kept abreast with it. Not wishing to hinder the next generation's opportunity to embrace Christianity, some members left to worship in a more formal style but continued to support Owen through the changes.

After three years in our new house, our needs were changing. Our children were growing up, and we were financially secure. Owen's dad was in the hospital, and Owen purchased a new automatic Holden Barina for his mum. At the age of seventy-five, she passed her driver's licence, which made her independent and able to make those daily hospital visits. We were spending more time with Owen's mum, so together we learnt how to play indoor bowls and contract bridge, and we even went white baiting!

The many Vineyard conferences we had attended over the years helped to heal and mature us spiritually, and Owen and I went looking for a new challenge. If something that we are doing does not challenge us, then it does not change us; besides, it is always exciting to be around happening things and see plans come together!

Motivated by our dream to make a living off the land like other family members, we went in search of properties. Our long-term plan was to invest for our retirement, and Owen had enough farming experience to know that we needed to buy land that would produce an income. We took months searching and researching properties and crops for opportunities. Then our friendly land agent, Brendon Richards, suggested we look at a place in Upper Moutere. When I argued that it was too far from Richmond, he replied, 'It can be done in fifteen minutes.'

And he did it! He drove speedily through the inland route over the gently rolling road through the Moutere Hills and down into the village in the Moutere Valley.

PART 2

An Upper Moutere Farm

The vertically soaring steeple of the Lutheran church makes a grand entrance to the Upper Moutere village, which services about four thousand locals living in the community, a primary school, post office, general store, garage, and the oldest New Zealand pub, the Moutere Inn, built in 1850. We drove one kilometre past the village, turned left off the main road onto Kelling Road, and then went up the road 280 metres over a bridge that spanned the Moutere Stream and headed into the farm.

The owner greeted us warmly on arrival and was ready to take us on a circuit of the farm. The twenty-five acres of land were bounded on one side by the Moutere Stream, and well-established apple orchards were along the eastern fence line. We continued walking up the dirt road leading into a large barn, which doubled as the shearing shed and a home for the sparse farm equipment and freshly cut hay. We looked north from the barn, where a flock of sheep was grazing along the line of conifers that marked the farm boundary. As we passed an old tin walled cottage, Owen and I began to visualize its potential once the glass bottles and rubbish randomly scattered all around were removed.

Gorse and broom covered the surrounding area, but flat land leading down to the Moutere Stream was revealed when we looked over the bank. The property came with water rights to irrigate the small raspberry garden that grew in front of the cottage, said to produce twenty tons on a good year!

Moving back down the dirt track, we came to another shed, one we could drive a tractor or truck through, which was exactly what happened during the raspberry harvest. The old Massey Ferguson tractor and trailer loaded with freshly picked raspberries would be driven into the shed and unloaded into an internal room, between the two dirt floor garages where the raspberries were sorted and then packed into fifteen-kilogram boxes before being sent to the Raspberry Marketing Committee.

As soon as we stepped on to the twenty hectares of land, we loved it – and that was without even thinking about a house! We were prepared to make the tin-walled cottage our home, but to our surprise and delight, we saw beyond the shed an attractive white, split-stone, boomerang-shaped house built around the 1960s. It had three bedrooms, a large laundry near the backdoor, a shower, a walk-in pantry across from the kitchen, and a small bathroom. The large lounge had an open fireplace and ranch sliders that exited out onto a raised concrete patio, from which one could capture glimpses through the undergrowth of what had once been a very attractive landscaped, circular driveway with an overgrown, neglected fernery in its far corner. The house, the grounds, and the farm had an air of despair and hopelessness about it. Two previous owners had not been able to make a living off the property, and now the present owner had come to the end of his resources and was caught in the same trap.

We had been looking at different properties, but none had felt as inspiring or offered as much potential as this one. Owen and I felt an emotional connection to the land, and by the end of the tour, we could hardly contain our excitement as we dreamed of the property's potential and the gratifying challenge it presented to us.

Our two Richmond properties sold by December 1987, and we moved onto the farm mortgage free and owning two vehicles. We became, the proud owners of a small flock of sheep, two goats, an old sheepdog named Tweep, and some hens that kept pooping all over the veranda. There was also an old red 135 Massy Ferguson tractor, and a rundown raspberry garden with a couple of rows of nectarine trees.

Then from the safety of the farmhouse that year, we watched the owner and his team work hard to harvest the raspberries, knowing that next year it would be our turn.

Kelling Road in 1990 with our house and land in the foreground.

A Taste of Country

We received a warm welcome from our neighbours, and with the frequently held street and dinner parties, we quickly became acquainted with them. The Thedins lived on the main road corner and grew peas for a vegetable processing company. Graeme Smeaton, a third-generation fruit farmer with a long history of raspberry growing, now had a well-established apple orchard and packing shed. He lived next door. Ivan Evans, a boysenberry grower, lived further up the road in an A-frame house, and next to him lived Bruce Wilson, an ex-teacher turned apple grower. Toss Woollaston, a well-known New Zealand painter, lived across the road on his apple orchard. He worked in a purpose-built studio set on a rise that overlooked the picturesque Moutere Valley with a magnificent view of the church steeple, which he loved. Sadly, he passed away in 1998, eleven years after we had taken up residency on Kelling Road.

It was summer when we moved onto the farm, and with our paddocks flush with grass, it was cut for hay and then left to dry before baling. Unfortunately, the day it was baled and ready for storage, the weather closed in, and we were anxious that it would not be stored before the rain ruined it all. Then as the rain began to fall, Graham Smeaton from next door pulled into the paddock in his red Ute, and he sprang into action by throwing the hay aboard. The hay was stored away in double quick time.

Helping to bring in the hay was only the first of the many times that Graeme came with his equipment to help us. My mother and father often came to stay. On one occasion she and I decided to rake up the gorse, cut along the boundary fence. We must have looked absurd to our country neighbours as we scratched away at this five-hectare paddock with our hand rakes dragging the gorse into burning piles. So it was not long before Graeme arrived well prepared with a back blade on his tractor, and in a very short time, he pushed the gorse into two big piles in the middle of the paddock, ready for burning.

After clearing the gorse, there remained a row of toe toes, giant tussock grasses with large creamy flower plumes on tall stems, standing erect down the middle of the paddock. Graeme offered to remove them. For ornamental reasons Owen had them replanted around the pond in the next paddock, where they added an eye-catching feature to the landscape. Although in years to come, they provided a nesting place for the birds that were always ready to feast on the raspberries during the season, Owen remained steadfast in his desire to retain the picturesque landscape, and the toe toes stayed.

Another day when Owen and I were using spades to dig up the rows of raspberry canes from in front of our house, ready to replant, Graeme again came to our rescue and arrived on his tractor. Attached to his tractor this time was a ripper that created a furrow, and the raspberries were dug up lickety-split!

Throughout the season, Graeme instructed Owen on growing raspberries. He had agreed to do our spraying, because we had no equipment, and he talked to Owen about harvesting an autumn crop. The new canes fruit about the end of March and continue until the frosts come in May, but if the bud moth gets into the canes and burrows in, nipping off the flower bud (which bears the fruit), there will be no crop. We had first-hand experience of that when Graham, who was one of the few orchardists able to grow an autumn crop, found leaf damage in our garden. He literally ran the half kilometre to his farm, jumped on his sprayer, and was at work in a very short time, spraying our patch of raspberries. If he had waited until the grubs were visible, it would have been too late – they would have already nipped out the fruit buds.

With Graeme's help that first year on the farm, we had the thrill of picking our first few raspberries, the autumn crop, which because of their long and slow ripening are the tastiest berries and make the best jam!

Faith Put to the Test

After enjoying a wonderful summer holiday on the farm, Owen and I reluctantly returned to work, back to Henley School in Richmond for me and to Cooper Webbleys for Owen. Our farm boundaries were lined with gorse, one of the most widely recognized agricultural weeds in New Zealand, so when Owen expressed his desire to clear it, Graeme put us in touch with Les Krammer, an experienced bulldozer driver who, although close to seventy, still did maintenance work on Graeme's orchard. Les was able to borrow Merv Laureen's bulldozer, and he made an immediate start to clear our boundary fences, much to the delight of our neighbours.

Les loved clearing the land of broom and gorse. I watched in awe at the confident way he handled and manoeuvred that tank-like machine, clearing the gorse, scraping and mounding the soil in order to reveal the productive land beneath. He worked joyfully like a kid with a new toy.

After almost two weeks of working on the job every day, Les had only one paddock left to disc before he finished – but sadly, that did not happen. Owen and I came home from work that day and stood and talked in front of the house, looking out over the river and enjoying the country scene. Owen said, 'I see Les's car there, but I don't hear the bulldozer.'

After speaking those words, Owen's walk turned into a jog as he raced down towards the barn. I trailed behind.

By the time I had joined Owen at the top of the bank, he had already looked down the track behind the barn, and with a tremor in his voice he turned to me and said, 'Don't come any further. Just go and get Graeme.'

I identified with horror the message that those words conveyed, and without hesitation I ran the distance to the house. I banged on the back door for what seemed like an eternity. Graeme came to the door, and I said, 'Could you come? Les has had an accident.'

Graeme let out a distressed groan, as if he expected the worst shouted to his wife Sarah to ring the fire brigade and was down at the accident scene within minutes. The fire brigade arrived immediately afterwards.

After the Labour Department investigations, the conclusion was that Les had come back from his lunch break about three o'clock and jumped on the bulldozer with the discs in tow. While driving down the track behind the barn, he'd lost control in the rough terrain, and the dozer had rolled over the bank, crushing him beneath. His sons, who were qualified heavy machinery drivers, came and examined the site. They were satisfied that it was an accident and no one was to blame.

It was a very difficult time for us, knowing that Les had lost his life while working on our farm. I wanted to run from the place and questioned what we were doing there.

As a tribute to Les, Mev Laureen came and finished bulldozing the last paddock before taking the bulldozer away. He simply said, 'Les would have liked that.'

It took Owen and me some time to recover from Les's death. I wanted to sell up and go, because I questioned whether clearing a piece of land was worth it. I had no knowledge of farm accidents until people came in the hopes of offering some comfort. They told me about the horrific accidents that had happened some years before, on their farms. The proverb 'Shared grief is half the sorrow' might comfort for a time, but I found some things about living in the country very difficult.

Graeme was able to organize the purchase of a house for Mrs Krammer, and she moved from the mill house to Stoke. She would call into the market stand in Nelson quite often to collect fresh raspberries from us for her jam making. The mill houses have been removed now, and there is no longer any visible sign of them having ever been there at the bottom of the Moutere Hill, as the chapter of Ted Krammar's life closed.

A Name for Our Farm

In 1986, New Zealand faced a time of social change. Owen's co-workers talked about the necessity of getting rid of Christian values in the schools. Upon hearing this, Owen decided it was time to shake the dust from his feet and leave the Department of Labour, where his newfound Christianity had no place. He had become frustrated with the pointless political activity of trying to motivate people to work who had neither the ability nor the inclination to do so. Therefore when an employment opportunity came from Bob Cooper, a local joiner, to set up a recently purchased refacing franchise business, Owen jumped at it.

Most people are happy with the layout of their kitchen and may simply want to update or change its colour. Refacing enables them to keep the layout, save thousands of dollars, and still have a high-quality finished kitchen. The cabinet gables, skirting boards, doors, and drawer fronts are removed and replaced with a new colour or product of the customer's choice, and of course a new bench top made by Bob's firm. Owen designed and printed pamphlets, and he advertised in the local papers. He set up the necessary records and then became busy with quotes and installations.

However, when we moved to the farm, things went quiet and Owen took the opportunity to buy the franchise and work the business from home. He purchased the necessary machinery from Woodworkers World, concreted the floor of the garage, and set up his joinery workshop, tailoring the joinery business to fit in with farm chores. We continued advertising through the newspaper and with brochures, and we even set up a display unit in the internal room of our garage for people to view.

Spare time on the farm saw Owen experimenting with his new woodworking tools, and I should have anticipated what happened next, but it took me completely by surprise. Using the newly purchased router, he had made a sign for the entrance to our farm. I arrived home from work the day that he made it, and he proudly paraded it in front of me. It was a white painted board, shaped and stylized like the wings of a dove in descending flight, with 'Anathoth' neatly carved out and painted in bright red letters on the white background. He even offered an explanation by saying that while reading the Bible, the name Anathoth had leapt out at him, and he had told himself, 'That's what I'll call our farm.'

He did not know how to pronounce it or what it meant, only that he had a peace about it. He liked the effective way it stylized and flowed across the arch-shaped board, much like the 1960s Ponderosa ranch in the television western *Bonanza*. He proudly held the sign aloft and asked me what I thought of that as a name for our farm.

I took one look at that sign, and without saying anything, I continued my walk into the house. Owen decided that this was not a nod of approval, so he carefully stored the sign in the shed, behind the freezer.

At least three months passed before I felt comfortable about the name on that sign, but knowing what it meant to Owen, I finally agreed. In no time at all, Owen had that sign pulled out from behind the freezer and swinging between two posts embedded in the garden, at the entrance to our driveway.

Anathoth means answered prayer, and it was to become the answer to Owen's prayer. Anathoth is pronounced ana-tot; the h is silent. As with Jeremiah, so it has been with Owen: a promise of restoration, of land and lives. Belief in God is a matter of faith – believing without knowing – and this gave Owen confidence about what he was doing with his life.

In all the years on the farm, the significance of Anathoth and its meaning when the going got tough kept inspiring us and lightened our burden. Owen would look over the bank down the valley and say, 'Well, Lord, if you want me to be here, then I know we will get through this difficulty.' Then he worked on in faith that it would be so with the goal always in sight.

First Phase

The twenty-year-old Marcy raspberries, already growing on the farm, covered about one hectare. To improve their productivity, one of the first things Owen did was change the irrigation system, from the existing overhead sprinklers to trickle irrigation. The new system he used dripped the water slowly through the pipes into the roots of the plants, saving on water and fertilizer. Added to this was Owen's care and attention to spraying, fertilizing, and specific instructions on how many canes per metre to leave when pruning, which meant he was able to get maximum production levels from the small area of existing plantings.

About June that year, my nephew John Purcell came back from England for a visit, bringing with him his partner, Helen, and a friend. They had spent some time with family on the farm in Whataroa and needed some money to visit the North Island before returning home. Owen quickly sprang into action and organized some raspberry planting on the two river gardens, which they managed to achieve in a couple of days before they left for their tour of the North Island. These were the first of the new plantings made over the next seven years, and it produced good crops in the first year of production. Unfortunately, Owen experimented by spraying out the early suckers in the spring, on advice he had been given from Nigel Warnes, another raspberry grower. One garden died out, and the second river garden was washed away when the river changed its course during a flood in 1994. Owen had more success with the raspberry gardens grown on the clay soil above the river loam.

The residents left on the farm to be cared for when we purchased were a hundred border leister ewes, two 'ancient' rams, and an aged sheepdog named Tweep. The rams just managed to service the flock the first year, but Owen managed to achieve only 90 per cent lambing. Unlike our neighbour, he was not satisfied with this because he was aiming for 100 per cent. The following year he purchased a younger ram and began the breeding program to improve our flock. He spent time tending the sheep and seldom called on the sheepdog to move them from one paddock to the next. The sheep came to know his voice and would willingly follow him. For the first few years on the farm, we enjoyed the seasonal work of lambing, planting, and pruning and harvesting our raspberry crop. Then as the raspberry plantings increased, so did our workload, and we found that during harvesting time, the sheep became neglected, so eventually they had to go.

In our very first raspberry season, with the help of pickers, we were able to take off a very small harvest of five tons – a long way short of the twenty tons talked about when we'd purchased the farm!

We sent our crop to the Raspberry Marketing Committee, who under government regulations had compulsory purchase. The picking costs were ninety cents a kilogram, and a dollar to grow, but we were not to receive a payment from the Raspberry Marketing Committee for two years – and it was less than a dollar a kilogram!

Struggling Through

Owen's Renoface work and my teaching job supported us through the first raspberry harvest. But the following year, I had taken leave from teaching, and with no payment for last year's raspberry crop and no orders in place or prospective clients waiting in the wings for the newly purchased refacing company, we needed an alternative idea for marketing. We decided to find potential customers by taking the set of impressive mobile Renoface display boards into the Nelson Market and demonstrate what the existing kitchen cupboards would look like when refaced.

On our first visit, Owen impressed me with his sales skills that he had gained years earlier when selling insurance and encyclopaedias. He had confidence in the Renoface system and was persuasive about the services he had to offer. I could see he enjoyed building strong relationships with people, and he gave the impression that he was having a ball. Potential customers responded to the visual display and the offer of a free measure and quote. After a few weeks, new orders kept him in work for the next few months.

I become bored while listening to Owen's repetitious sales pitch, so the following week I decided to make and sell some raspberry jam, thinking that it would help defray market expenses and add to our meagre income. These were the early days in the Nelson Market when food regulations permitted such activities.

I made about ten pots of raspberry jam in recycled glass jars with cellophane lids, and I counted myself very fortunate when it all sold. The next week I made twice as many pots, and they sold too.

Owen was watching the sale of the jam and the eagerness with which the customers purchased it, so he decided to help me make the jam. With Owen stirring the cooked jam, we were able to double our output. We sold out every week but still did not satisfy the market! Even the woman who worked the stall of a local fruit grower who made jam came to our stall and bought our raspberry jam, because as she said, 'Yours is much better.'

After having achieved enough interest in the Renoface system by June that year, and after having turned our meagre supply of raspberries into jam, we finished our spell at the Nelson Market. Because it created a good cash flow, we returned in December with our fresh punnets of raspberries.

Selling our raspberries in the Market

Farm Life

By changing from overhead sprinklers to trickle irrigation, Owen had improved the health of the raspberry plants, but it increased the cost of development. That meant we could not increase our plantings as quickly as we would have liked, and with the plants taking three years to mature and produce fruit, the return was very slow. I had taken time out from teaching, so without my wage we struggled financially that year, although somehow we managed to increase our plantings.

Tim in the Sprayer

When Graeme was no longer able to do our spraying, Owen went looking to buy spraying equipment. He wanted an enclosed cab sprayer. He eventually found a second-hand one used on lemons, which he reckoned would be suitable for our raspberries. After raising finance, he became the proud owner of what came to be affectionately known as Noddy.

When the Raspberry Marketing Committee announced that no payment of harvested raspberries was to be paid out until the berries were sold, we quickly realized that harvesting raspberries and selling to the committee was not going to produce a reliable income. After discovering our success with past raspberry jam sales, we reckoned that we might be able to capitalize on the customer demand and generate some of our own income. Processing our fruit was not what I'd had in mind when we'd moved to the farm, but adding value to the crop and converting it into jam appeared to be the obvious solution and a financial lifeline!

When we returned to the Nelson Market with fresh berries in December, we stayed selling in the market long after the raspberry season to sell our jam. The bulk of our harvest for the year had gone to the Raspberry Marketing Committee once again, but we had packed into three-kilogram lots about one and a half tons of our harvest, and we froze them in large second-hand chest freezers ready for jam making.

The jam only took up a small space on our stall at the market, so we began to lend out our Christian books. The books enabled us to build relationships and connect with people, which increased our customer base.

By this time, Owen and I had developed a system for the jam-making process. I cooked the first batch of jam, and he would stir it for twenty minutes while it cooled and thickened. It cooled quicker by sitting the jam pan in a tub of cold water. Then I would cook the next one, and when that was ready, he would stir and cool it while I filled the jars.

At first we used recycled glass jars, but Owen did not think they looked attractive enough, so we used clear plastic drinking cups with lids. The cups did not seal and so could not preserve the jam in the long term. Fortunately, the jam was so tasty that our customers consumed it within a week and then returned for more! These containers were very brittle and broke easily. However, the visual appearance of the jam, which showed off well in the plastic cup, was a distinct selling advantage because it translated into customers' perception of taste and flavour.

Saturday morning at the market was an enjoyable social activity and became a way of life for us over the next twelve years.

Meeting Canadian visitors at the market
with our Christian books and jam.

Raspberry Marketing Regulations

After being tied into government regulations, for the disposal of our fruit had proven unsuccessful, Owen could see no other way of receiving a secure and regular stream of income than by making jam. At the very least, we would have more control on our return.

He began to search for ways around the existing government regulations regarding the sale of raspberries that would allow us to manufacture our raspberries into jam. He knew that government employees worked on the principle that all the boxes had to be ticked, so with that in mind, he reckoned the best way to find out what the legislation said, in order to put the jam business on a legal footing, was to get a copy of the act and read it. He knew that he was legally forced to sell his raspberries to the regional Nelson Raspberry Marketing Committee, but he discovered he was able to become a buyer of raspberries, manufacture jam, and sell it.

After negotiating with the Nelson Raspberry Marketing Committee, the committee decided that if Owen continued to pay the eight cents per kilogram levy imposed on the crop he kept and used for jam making, they would deem the crop to have met the legal requirements, which was to buy and sell through the committee. He was in every sense of the word paying a penalty for using his own fruit, but Owen was a very honest man and complied.

The committee continued receiving our eight cent per kilogram levy from our berries for the next nine years. When our entire crop of seventy-five tons was going into jam, it meant we were paying a penalty equating to six thousand dollars the first year, and a total of twenty-eight thousand dollars in the years following. This was before deregulation came in 1999. That amount of capital invested in our farm would have given us a far better return!

After making contact with the committee, in order to look after his interests, Owen became a member of the Nelson Raspberry Committee and the New Zealand Raspberry Marketing Council. In June 1998 the Asia-Pacific Economic Cooperation (APEC) required a level playing field with free trade, so a review of the regulatory structure of the New Zealand raspberry industry in consultation with growers took place. The review endorsed the disadvantage to newcomers and stated that the regulations had given benefits to existing growers over new entrants. The contribution of the raspberry industry, once a valuable fruit export, had diminished as a result.

We were among the number of the new growers referred to in the document, because of the fixed production quotas and the penalties imposed on any initiative farmers might have in disposing of their fruit in a profitable manner. However, this was only one of the reasons for the demise of the industry. Labour laws in successive governments removed the incentive for people to perform when doing contract piecework, making it difficult for us to take on pickers. We were continually harassed by the department. Added to this was an inaccurate diagnosis of bushy dwarf virus by plant scientists and the rumour that it was decimating raspberry gardens.

When Owen heard that the disease itself was unidentifiable, he had doubts about the conclusions reached. He was told that the yellowing of the leaves was what the experts observed and concluded to be bushy dwarf virus. Owen was a keen observer of the behaviour of his plants, and he was not satisfied with the diagnosis of the experts, so his ability and determination to solve problems by gathering and evaluating accurate information kicked in. When the leaves on our raspberry bushes were yellowing, Owen sent them away to a laboratory for analysis, and the results showed a deficiency in magnesium. From his experience, while making aluminium alloys at the Tiwai smelter, Owen remembered that a boron flux was used to precipitate out magnesium in the manufacture of metal. Therefore, he suspected that the use of boron as a fertilizer was inhibiting the uptake of magnesium and poisoning the plants. The symptoms of boron poisoning were the same as the symptoms attributed to bushy dwarf virus.

After coming to this conclusion, Owen always ensured that the fertilizer company added no boron to our berry mix. Only then did our plants return to a healthy green colour, and the crumbly fruit disappeared.

Owen often gave this information to other raspberry growers, but to no avail, because the 'advisers' were still recommending boron as an additive.

The year that Harvey Hall, a scientist from the DSIR, looked at our garden and told Owen that he had this virus in his garden, Owen asked if the virus could be seen. Harvey replied no, adding only the effect was seen, with leaves turning yellow and the fruits being smaller than normal or crumbly at harvest time.

Owen did not wish to offend, but he tactfully replied, 'Give me some more of that, because I have just taken off one hundred tons of raspberries – the best year I have ever had.'

When we visited Scotland in 1994, we saw the same yellowing of the leaves that decimated their crop. They also called it bushy dwarf virus!

Disposal of Assets

When the government regulations ceased, the assets of the Raspberry Marketing Committee had to be disposed of, and the government regulatory body gave the instructions for their distribution as follows: 'Remaining assets were to be transferred to current growers in proportion to the quantity of raspberries they had marketed through the committee during the ten-year period ending 30 June 1999.'

The biggest growers in the district at this time were Owen, and Nigel Warnes from Tapawera. Owen had continually paid his levies over the year and was legally qualified as one of the biggest growers. Both growers were entitled to the largest share, amounting to fifty thousand dollars each! To Owen's surprise, a letter came from the committee to say that he would not be receiving a payout.

Our lawyer, David Maze, acknowledged that we had a legal right to a share of the board's assets, and he was ready to make application to the court to claim the fifty thousand as set out in the legislation. Before it could proceed, however, we were paid a rare visit by a neighbouring grower intent on delivering a message. He sat in our lounge after being made welcome, turned his head, and looked at our raspberry plantings. To our surprise, he suddenly blurted out, 'Owen, you are not a raspberry grower.'

Quite taken aback and not realizing where this conversation was going, I pointed to the raspberries growing in the paddock and asked him, in not too kindly a tone, what he thought those plants out there were.

Our raspberry garden

Owen, his usual quiet self, waited for the punchline. The neighbour was still plucking up courage to focus on the real reason for his visit. He ignored my reply and continued to deliver his message. 'Owen, if you take your claim for the Raspberry Committee assets any further with a court case, the other farmers who are getting a share of the assets will all put in three thousand dollars, which is the amount they will get, to oppose your claim. It will cost you fifty thousand dollars to oppose them – about the amount you are entitled to.'

Sickened by the thought of court action against the very growers we had worked alongside, all in order to claim what was legally ours, we dropped the case. The Tapawera grower received the largest pay out, and small amounts went to other growers. We moved on from that unsavoury episode.

In hindsight and with the experience we had some years later, we now realize that by not pursuing claims in some manner, ruthless, money-hungry individuals would take advantage of us.

An Unexpected Calamity

Owen had kept in contact with John Mullis, director of Christian Advance Ministries, a non-denominational ministry established to serve Christian renewal in the mainline churches of New Zealand over the years. John asked Owen to organize a venue for a two-day conference in our hometown for a visiting Vineyard American pastor, Ron Ford, and his team. Owen was excited about the visit, so when he heard that they required a vehicle to carry music equipment, he offered to provide and drive our 1987 Mitsubishi Ute. His offer for the vehicle was accepted, but to Owen's disappointment they already had a designated driver, someone on the tour who was going back to the States to train in ministry.

When the time came for the tour to start, we met their nominated tour driver at the Nelson airport. ready to deliver the Ute into his care. To my surprise, Owen asked if he had a current driver's licence.

'Yes, I have all that.' came the prompt reply, as I would have expected. He avoided any small talk, and after accepting the cut lunch I had made for the twelve-hour journey, he seemed anxious to be on his way. He jumped in the Ute, said a quick goodbye, and was off in a flash, heading for Invercargill to meet up with the team that had flown in. After a couple of meetings, they drove north to Queenstown.

Owen and I had recently travelled to Invercargill for his niece's wedding, and we'd driven back to Christchurch via Queenstown to visit my mother, who lived there. From Queenstown we had journeyed through the Lindis Pass, which in winter is a renowned spot for notorious accidents caused by black ice, especially by drivers inexperienced with these conditions. The black ice comes during a bitterly cold week in the south, with temperatures in some areas dropping below 20 degrees Celsius.

Colin Perry, from Wellington, was the navigator on the tour and drove the van carrying the team. Ron Ford travelled with the driver in our Ute, which carried the musical equipment. Owen had warned Colin about the black ice on the Lindis Pass and asked him for an undertaking not to take our vehicle through there; they should use the alternative route.

Four days into their tour, a phone call came to say that their driver had rolled our vehicle on black ice while going through the Lindis Pass. Fortunately for its occupants, when the Ute hit the black ice and rolled, the metal frame set above the deck acted like a set of skis, sliding the upturned Ute gracefully and gently along the highway, depositing it down a low grassy bank along the side of the road upside down. Ron Ford and the driver were left hanging upside down by their seat belts, badly shaken but unhurt. Their good fortune was due to the fact that they had been protected by the Ute's metal frame.

After the accident, the group had piled the music equipment into the van, abandoned the Ute, and travelled on to the nearest township, Omarama, about twenty minutes away. They phoned Owen to give him the news.

Owen was concerned about the abandonment of the vehicle on this lonely stretch of road, so he sprang into action and rang the local garage at Omarama. After explaining the situation to the owner, who fortunately was sympathetic to Owen's dilemma, the man lost no time in retrieving our vehicle. Then after notifying our insurance company, the Ute was promptly towed out for transportation to the Mitsubishi dealers in Nelson, ready to be rebuilt.

The group continued their tour and eventually arrived in Nelson. After meeting up with them, we learnt first-hand how the accident had happened. However, it was not until the meeting started that the driver of the Ute pulled Owen aside to give him some bad news. 'Owen, there is something I have to tell you.'

Owen's heart sank as he guessed the worst. 'Owen I have wronged you. I don't have a driver's licence. In fact, I have never had a licence, although I have driven vehicles.'

Owen was shocked at the betrayal. When Ron Ford heard the news, he immediately sent the guy, whose prospects in ministry were now at an end, on the next plane back to Auckland.

Immediately Owen went to our insurance company and explained the situation. They were very sympathetic and agreed to continue with the arrangements, and they'd bill us accordingly. This was our farm vehicle, and it was difficult to be without it. Financing the repairs would be challenging to say the least, and it would take weeks to rebuild.

The touring group continued on their way, and ongoing communication with Christian Advance Ministries and the Vineyard Christian Fellowship in America saw both organisations contributing to the full cost of the restoration of our Ute.

Owen with our restored ute

Backpackers for Farm Work

Our faithful pensioners from Motueka continued to come each year to pick our autumn crop, but close to the end of our second season, with fewer berries to pick, they quit. While there were berries still on the bushes, I was determined to pick every last one, even without help!

As I finished up in the field for the day and was making my way back to the shed, I became overwhelmed by the enormity of the task that lay before me. In desperation I looked heavenward, as one did in such circumstances, and I uttered loudly, 'Please send someone to help.'

Lo and behold, as I rounded the corner of the shed, to my surprise I saw Owen talking to a poorly dressed young man on a bicycle. His eyes were red, and he looked dusty and dishevelled. He was asking Owen for work. Owen decided he did not like the look of him and was busy telling him there was no work.

I pulled Owen to one side and in a soft voice queried, 'I've just asked for help. Do you think he has been sent?'

Hearing my message, Owen relented and asked the young man if he wanted to stay and pick berries. He said his name was Christian Schueyer to which Owen quickly asked, 'And are you one?'

Christian turned out to be an Austrian on his overseas working holiday, and he stayed working with us for six weeks. He shared with us that his father had died when he was young, and after his time abroad, he was going home to accept the responsibility of looking after his mother and two younger siblings. Six weeks later, he continued on his cycle tour of the South Island and returned later that year to stay with us again. He wrote from home a couple of times expressing his gratitude for the mentoring he had received from Owen. Christian became the first of many backpackers who stayed in the house with us or camped on the farm and used the facilities in the house.

Once we had four Israeli boys who taught us how to pronounce Anathoth, but most who came to our area were Germans and Austrians. An interesting older woman, who was a French underground train driver, came to cook jam, but instead she ended up baking chocolate cakes for Owen!

When we were in need of more raspberry pickers, Owen would pick up backpackers from hostels, roadsides, or the market and offer them a bed and paid work.

Two Canadian backpackers we met at the Nelson Market were sisters, Kim and Lauren Bayard from Maryland. They jumped at the chance of staying a couple of nights on the farm while Owen and I had a two-day rest in a cottage in the Marlborough Sounds. That was my fiftieth birthday present – a holiday of rest and a few days away from work! It was much more interesting than my forty-fifth birthday present, moving the chook house down onto the river flat and away from the house.

A Nuisance Averted

By the next raspberry season, we were employing one hundred raspberry pickers a day over the six weeks of harvest. Now we really knew we were into the berry harvest. Every day the supervisor in the raspberry garden would tell me how many pickers I needed to put into the field each day. At the height of the season, it would be as many as150.

Shortly before the commencement of the season, the Inland Revenue sent all growers notification that they were introducing a new form, which would require us to record the employees' commencement and cessation dates. This was going to prove to be a very difficult exercise; some growers called it an impossible task. Raspberry pickers worked on contract and chose when to turn up for work, which was off and on during the season. After orchardists raised these concerns, Owen made a protest to our local member of parliament, Nick Smith, who was an influential spokesperson for our local interests.

Nick put our case to Minister of Revenue Wyatt Creech and then forwarded us a copy of the letter he had sent. The body of the letter explained how the extra paperwork needed to complete this IR66ES form was substantial, and small businesses would not be taking on new employees if the government kept burying them with additional paperwork, when the information had already been supplied on IR12/13. Thanks to Nick Smith's action, the new form was reviewed, and concessions were made for seasonal employers!

PART 3

A Commercial Kitchen, 1991

After selling berries and jam at the Nelson Market through two raspberry harvest seasons, demand for our raspberry jam kept growing, and by 1990 the potential was there for an increase in sales. We had a product that people wanted, and all we had to do was produce it and fill the gap in the market for a quality jam!

It was only when Owen discovered there were no regulations about adding value to the crop and converting it into jam that it looked like a goer. As he was sharing his vision of expanding the jam manufacturing with me, he realized that I was not exactly jumping up and down with joy over this newfound direction for our lives. I could not see myself giving up teaching to make raspberry jam full time. Nevertheless, survival on the farm and Owen's persuasive reasoning helped me to come to terms with our situation. Besides, a journey once started needed to be completed!

Our past experience with the Raspberry Marketing Committee's slow and low payments convinced us that the only course of action was to have some control in the marketing of our own berries, and this would only be possible if we made jam. We reckoned that if we did not take this course of action, we would be defeated financially, just like the last owners of the property.

With the volume of jam sales increasing and a decision made, Owen reckoned that it was time to legitimise our manufacturing by licensing a commercial kitchen. The lifestyle I had imagined was now quickly becoming a distant, unattainable dream, and a different reality began taking shape. Owen's vision and his motivating words reverberated in my head and kept me keen to move ahead and expand the jam sales. 'If you want to get out of the jam factory, you have to grow the business.' However, to accomplish his vision of turning our raspberries into jam, things had to change – and they did! Owen became involved with jam making, and by working together, we were able to double our output.

This new direction meant abandoning the Renoface franchise, as well as upgrading and refurbishing the showroom as a commercial kitchen. In the short time we had been on the farm, this internal room between the two garages had gone through various upgrades, from a raspberry sorting room to a poolroom for teenagers to a Renoface display room. Now, it was to becoming a jam factory. In preparation for such an event, Owen had already consulted the health inspector, who confirmed that the room could be brought up to standard for minimal cost.

Before he went ahead with any other development, Owen needed to know from the council whether the proposed usage was within the planning requirements for the area. He knew there were general building requirements along with local council and government regulations that covered what one could and could not do. In June 1990

Owen wrote out an application to the council to find out if our jam making was permissible.

His vision at that time was not very ambitious: a microbusiness, something very small that could generate an income for us. He wrote that he had been conducting feasibility studies on further processing part of our farm produce, raspberries. However, to continue with this experiment, he needed to manufacture sufficient quantities to accurately test the local market and refine the production process. He desired to establish a small home occupation processing three to five tons of berries per year from our own stocks of frozen berries, kept in cold storage in Richmond. He did not envisage employing staff in this process, because there was only about two days per week work involved in producing this quantity. We would have minimal jam sales from the premises in conjunction with fresh berry sales during the season, because the jam was to be sold through local shops and the Nelson Market. We already had a large off-road metalled parking facility 240 square metres in area.

Applying for the factory licence was not a speedy process. It took until the August the following year before the application to manufacture and retail jam in a rural A zone was even heard. The council replied by sending us a copy of their hearing procedures.

First, we needed to apply to the council for a specified departure, which then allowed the council to consider uses not provided for in the district scheme. The council in turn advertised our application and sent copies of the application to those people it considered to have a greater interest than the public – generally, neighbours.

Our application was open to objections for twenty-one days from the date of notification. This process took weeks! After the closing date for the objections had passed and no protest was recorded, the council gave formal consent for the factory inspection to take place, followed by registration. The application fee was one thousand dollars and covered advertising, site inspection, report writing, and hearing expenses. Then we were finally and successfully through the registration process.

The food industry regulations demanded that the garages on either side of the factory, used as storerooms, have concrete floors and plywood-lined walls. The floor of the proposed commercial kitchen was plastered to make it smooth and level for the coved vinyl, as the regulations required.

Owen became troubled at the setup costs to meet the regulations mounting. He reckoned after calculating the ongoing costs of working through the red tape, administration, compliance, and matters relating to future business that we needed to generate enough sales from the jam to provide an income to support five families before getting anything for ourselves. This gave him plenty of motivation to grow the business. We courageously pressed on as the expenditure went up!

A heavy-duty dishwasher, a stainless steel tub, and a hand-washing sink were needed in the factory. Owen made a savings when he acquired a stainless steel butcher's table from a shopkeeper in exchange for wooden display shelves he'd made himself. Gas burners, jam pans, and expensive digital timers were more items on the equipment list. The jam pans we needed were heavy base pans with low-sided, wide saucepans for gas cooking. They were in short supply and were very expensive, but we did manage to buy two from a local hardware store.

Whenever we visited a town, we would search the stores for jam pans and were able to purchase six more to increase our cooking. Later, as new factories were built, each one required at least thirty jam pans to rotate for their cooking. To fulfil our requirements, Owen contacted the pan manufacturer in Wellington who imported the circles from Wales. The manufacturer required a minimum order of a hundred, which was no problem for us because we then sold our extras to other factories. Years later, when the manufacturer threatened to sell the tool that made the pans, Owen paid him five thousand dollars and took ownership of the tool!

By the time we were ready to commence cooking in our registered kitchen on three gas burners, Owen had worked out a cost-effective system designed to increase production and produce a consistent jam. Every action he took had been documented, every process of the jam making was timed, and different amounts of raspberries were tested to establish the maximum weight that processed efficiently without losing the quality of the jam. Installed digital timers assisted in monitoring the process.

Using thawed frozen fruit, the raspberries took twenty minutes coming to a boil and needed only occasional stirring to ensure all the fruit was cooked. With the sugar added, the berries returned to the boil in five minutes. Then after boiling for fifteen minutes, the jam came off the gas and cooled in a water bath essential for raspberry jam, because the seeds will sometimes separate when potted hot.

By placing ten minutes between each batch, and the jam not requiring constant attention, Owen was able to have three pots cooking at one time. He had experience with the training within industry method, which was how he trained me (and later, other jam makers). This training system, based on the same method used to train air force pilots during the Second World War, was tell, show, and then allow trainees to try, monitoring and correcting as they learnt. The cooking system was only efficient if workers followed training instructions to the letter. Stirring the uncooked berries to distribute the heat and responding to the timers were keys to maintaining these efficiencies. As employees gained experience, they could cook on up to nine burners at a time, and they later prided themselves on handling twelve burners installed years later in the new factory. By producing the jam efficiently, we were able to remain competitive in the market.

After the factory was set up and ready to go, I would come home from a day's teaching. Owen would have tea ready, and we would make jam until the late evening.

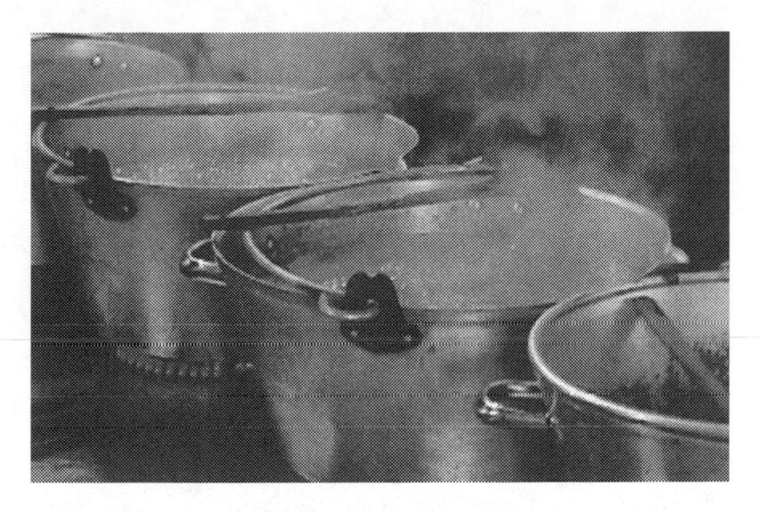

This photo was taken in the small factory, which started on three burners and increased to nine. This factory served us well until 1999, when it was replaced with a new twenty-four burner factory and freezer.

After all this expenditure, we were poised and ready for a jump in sales.

Market Readiness

The legal minimum fruit content for commercial jams is 40 per cent, and because manufacturers boost fruit percentage by using concentrated fruit juices and purees, people who enjoyed a tasty, full fruit jam have been obliged to make their own. When consumers first tasted our raspberry jam, they preferred it over other jams, and they even stopped making their own because, as they said, we did it so much better. Jam lovers promptly connect with the flavour and freshness of our raspberry jam. Owen's system of cooking guaranteed its quality and consistency; like McDonald's, it was always the same.

With the success we were having selling our raspberry jam, Owen saw it as an opportunity to start a business. It was most opportune for us when Steve Olds from Tecpak Dunedin, a plastic manufacturer, approached us in the Nelson Market, to promote the mussel pot his company made. When Steve saw the container Owen had his jam in – clear, brittle plastic drinking cups with their clip on lids – he suggested the mussel pot as an alternative. He told us the pots were sterilized, watertight, airtight, and light, and therefore more economical to transport than glass. They were also recyclable.

The secret to a good homemade jam is to evaporate off the liquid by cooking in small batches, because when the liquid is boiled off, no pectin or jelling agents or chemicals are needed to make it set. Mould becomes the only problem in keeping the jam. In Grandma's day, the jam was put into glass jars, and a cellophane cover soaked in water was placed over the jar with a rubber band, allowing the heat of the jam to dry the cellophane and seal it. If mould grew on the jam, it was scraped off before eating. At times the jam was sealed with a wax coating. Nowadays, gas is used to fill the gap between the jam and the lid.

Steve was offering us a plastic pot that we could burp to let the air out of, which sealed the jam and prevented spoiling. The plastic, airtight container proved to be exactly what we needed. A new and innovative idea for packaging jam was birthed as Owen became the first to launch jam in a plastic pot.

When Owen was designing the jam pot label, he was able to recall the marketing principles he had learnt when studying church growth with John Wimber. Something that is working should be adopted rather than adapted! He began applying these same successful principles of church planting to the jam label. The first principle is based on the understanding that in today's world, there are so many hundreds of messages coming at us that we have developed a highly sensitive screening system preventing us from seeing most of these communications, because our minds cannot handle and process all the communications directed at us every day. The amount of information that was coming off the label had to be kept to a minimum.

The product needed to have a brand name to identify it for rebuying. Owen chose Anathoth, the name of our farm. Then he put the legal requirement, a list of the ingredients and nutritional values. He added to that the barcode for supermarket trading. The barcodes, required for retail products, are purchased and formatted by EAN, a non-profit, business-led association that manages a worldwide system of identification. The only unnecessary information put on the label was the promotional wording 'Pure and Natural', which Owen did not want to include but was convinced to do so by the printer. In retrospect, it was good advice because customers appreciated and sought food labelled pure and natural.

As well as reducing the written communication on the product, Owen put a greater emphasis on visibility. He chose to make the colour and attractive appearance of the product as visible as possible. People often judge a raspberry jam by its colour and the number of visible seeds. The jam pot's shape and appearance was important too. It had to be significantly different from all other products on the shelf to make it easily identifiable. That's what Steve's company, Tecpak, had given us. Of course, this principle s only an advantage, when there is a significantly better quality of product, which attracts the customers. When all your petrol comes out of the same refinery, you are best to have your label looking like everybody else's and attract people with gimmicks. These plastic pottles with their simple labels Owen designed created either a love or hate reaction with people. Customers loved the pot for its simple message, many uses, and recyclability. After our pot had been on the supermarket shelf for some time, I lost count of the number of times marketers and graphic designers approached Owen, saying that they would be more than willing to 'fix up' his packaging to make it more attractive and appealing. Owen tactlessly repealed each attack, because he was confident and more than happy with the way the label conveyed his values and his story. It worked for him, and after all if it ain't broke, why fix it?

For Owen, marketing a product was not an academic exercise, where you display your knowledge and ability through packaging and websites in the hope of attracting people to your product.

Owen stayed away from the accepted practice of deceit and allowed the quality and price of our product to be presented through the jam pot's simple, honest labelling and the customers' tasting of the product. His rational was, 'What you see is what you get!' If it's a pot of raspberry jam, it's a pot of raspberry jam.

The experience of eating the product was then limited to taste and nutritional effects. Experiencing these aspects of a product enabled customers to choose whether or not to buy it. This method of selling is absent of deceit, and when associated with a brand name, it will create lifetime customers. That is what happened with our Anathoth!

Owen found it easy to think out his approach at the start, and he did everything according to the book, considering and pre-planning the steps before taking action, just as he did when building our house. He set out his big goal and then broke it down into steps; the steps broke down into parts, and the parts broke down into details. Because he had identified his values as quality, efficiency, and service, and he had lived a value-driven lifestyle, it made it easy to govern his business practices. He reasoned every action that he took and never made a decision unless he had considered all the information available. He knew where he was going, so it was easy to take others there. If you have not been there before, how can you expect to take someone else?

We had a story to be told about our Anathoth brand. We shared with our customers how we came to name our farm, Anathoth, from the Bible's Jeremiah 32, and how it later came to be put on our jam pot. Our pot with its simply designed label, which people clearly connected with, helped them to choose between brands.

Owen was satisfied that through our plastic pot and simple labelling, he had effectively delivered and communicated our values in a memorable manner. With a meaningful point of difference, we had the opportunity to grow a strong brand.

Finance for a New Business

Financing a growing business can be a struggle for many an entrepreneur. As the raspberry season in the 1992–1993 season approached, Owen went to the bank for seasonal finance and working capital, in order to fund the future jam business. A new bank employee from the auditor's office in Wellington, who had recently joined the bank, visited our home and rejected Owen's proposal, ridiculing him in the process. With conviction he offensively declared, 'There is no way you are going to do what you predict you will do. You're dreaming!' He was of course talking about Owen's forecasted production and sales of raspberries and raspberry jam.

Owen took it all in his stride, but he was not satisfied with this employee's assessment, and he was unhappy with the rudeness of his approach. He contacted the general manager of Westpac in Nelson. The general manager apologized for the man's approach and manners, but he asked Owen if he would excuse him and go back to work with him. Apparently, he was just out of the auditor's office and was 'good at his job', but he lacked experience with business projects and had considerable learning to do in this area.

With finance for expansion of our jam business snubbed and relations with Westpac strained, we struggled through the raspberry season, and then Owen went shopping for a new lender. He chose the Auckland Savings Bank, the first New Zealand bank to introduce Internet banking (in 1997). Their manager, Brendon Forrest, guided Owen through their new procedures, and Owen selected a New Zealand company, Rees Easy, for his accounting programme.

Evolving Jam Sales

Our jam sales at the Nelson Market were growing as Owen had forecasted, and customers were saying, 'That's the best jam I've ever tasted. Give me another fix!'

Owen had fun selling in the market and had a repetitive, irresistible sales pitch, which would become a two-way conversation. He had responses like, 'It comes with money back guarantee if you are not satisfied.'

If people said they came from out of town, he would reply, 'It flies really well.' He'd demonstrate this by tossing a jam from one hand to the other. 'It even goes across the sea,' he'd add as he jiggled the pot in a straight line. Customers responded to the interaction.

It wasn't long before a local fruit and vegetable owner, Gerald Haycock, who also loved a good sales pitch, approached us about selling our raspberry jam in his shop. As fast as I was mouthing no, I heard Owen saying that it wouldn't be a problem. I did not foresee Owen's future ambition at this time, which was that Gerald's shop was to become the first of many outlets for our jam.

Gerald built relationships with his customers through his storytelling, so we should not have been surprised when one day he asked us to be quick about the delivery we were making. When Owen asked why, Gerald replied with amusement,

'I have a story about an old, grey-haired couple that make this homemade jam in the Moutere, and you certainly don't fit the bill!'

Owen's philosophy was to always grow the business, or else it would die. Because he found it so easy to identify what action was needed to grow the business, he thought that if he didn't do it, someone else would. In order to expand sales, he approached the local businesses, and we received abundant support. Our outlets grew: Richmond Night and Day, Arkrites, Tahuna, Combined Rural Traders, Watson's Keystores Richmond and Alistair Clarke's Keystore, and Motueka Market.

Alistair, who went on to expand his business by building the New World Motueka, was exceptionally helpful in promoting our jam. He would load up his trailer with raspberry jam and take it to a relative who owned Smith's Variety store in Milton, a farming district of two thousand people some fifty kilometres south of Dunedin. Smiths would then put a notice in their store: 'Raspberry Jam Arriving Wednesday.' Then customers would buy the jam by the box to stock up for the next three months, before the next lot arrived. How could anyone organize that kind of promotion? Alistair's trailer was then loaded with famous tasty, frost-chilled, Southland swedes to bring back to Motueka.

Customers got excited about the high quality of the raspberry jam made from local fruit. They wanted products that contained no pig fat, colouring, chemicals, stabilizers, thickeners, preservatives, and mysterious ingredients known only as 202, 631, or pectin, which took away the lovely natural fruit flavour.

When quizzed by the media about his growing market, Owen would say, 'We really can't predict the future, but building a brand and continuing to succeed is all about knowing our customers. Over time, we have earned their trust and confidence, and by continuing to provide a good, consistent product and service, we will ensure an increase in our sales.'

Our customers recommending the jam to their friends and neighbours became our most valuable marketing asset.

When visitors came to Nelson from different parts of New Zealand, they tried our jam and wanted to know where they could get more. Owen saw an opportunity for home delivery, so he set up a mail order delivery service with the newly established franchised business Fastways, a low-cost courier firm started in 1983. We were one of their first regular customers to use their fast-growing service, which expanded into Australia ten years later. One cook-up of jam fitted neatly into a five-kilogram white liver pail. We wrote the address on top, and it was then delivered door to door anywhere in New Zealand. To retain the colour and freshness of the jam, we recommended freezing it because the sugar content allowed the jam to remain free flowing, and therefore it was easy to scoop out a bowlful at a time.

A regular Wellington customer who used this service rang up one day and complained that his jam pail had not arrived. In tracking down the order, it was discovered that he had painters working at his house, so when the courier dropped off the white pail, they naturally thought it was more paint, and placed it beside all the other paint pots.

After realizing the mistake, the customer sent a photo of the labelled jam container surrounded by all the other white paint pots.

When sales extended nationwide, we began advertising the mail order service in a nationwide agriculture paper, *The Dairyman*. In the 1993 July issue a promotional article was written about how we were farmers promoting our joinery business at the Nelson Market when, after selling some pot of raspberry jam, the business snowballed into a demand for mail order. As the customers increased jam lovers wrote wonderful letters of thanks for producing a homemade jam, and they encouraged us with comments:

'The flavours remind me of my childhood, you know, when raspberries tasted like raspberries.'

'Many thanks for making shopping days a little nicer, because you took the trouble to make your product excellent.'

When Owen named our farm Anathoth, it had been a natural progression for him to put that name on our jam pot. How this name came to be there and what it meant to us became a great story to tell our customers when they asked (as they often did) for years to come. The name prompted Natalie Max to send us a card that read:

O Taste and see that the Lord is Good.
Psalm 34:8

I found this story behind the name Anathoth very interesting, and it's surprising where a label on a pottle of raspberry jam can lead to!

> Card making is my hobby, but I really like to think of it as my ministry, as I do it for the Lord. I know he helps me be creative. He certainly helps you to make delicious jam.

The card was beautiful, and the words inspired me each time I read them as I passed by its place on our mantelpiece.

An Embryonic Enterprise

At the same time our farming operation was emerging, after twenty-seven years teaching, I felt a desire to contribute to the Christian community by assisting the Reformed Church in fulfilling their ten-year ambition of establishing a Christian school in Nelson.

A hall at the All Saints Anglican Church in Nelson had become available, so I took up the challenging task of moving the incoming pupils from a home-schooling situation to a registered school – all in twelve months! The parents received one thousand dollars from the government for home schooling for the first child, six hundred dollars for the second, and a descending scale for each child thereafter. These fees were paid to the board, and the school's expenses were taken out. Along with members of the board and prospective parents, we renovated the hall and changed it into a suitable classroom.

Money was in short supply, so I collected out-of-date school journals, spelling books, dictionaries, and more from my teaching colleagues, as well as books and equipment necessary to implement the syllabus for the school to start in May 1990. Desks, chairs, and mats also found their way into the new classroom.

We started the school with five pupils, believing that it would grow. By the end of the term, we had nine, and the following year, after having achieved government registration, numbers increased to seventeen, which was enough for a sole charge school!

The first term of operation went very smoothly, but six weeks into the third term, I received word that my father had cancer of the oesophagus, and he was to have an operation in Invercargill. It was difficult to find a relieving teacher to take my place so that I could spend time with my parents, and all I managed was a long weekend. After the operation, my father came out of intensive care, had a relapse, and passed away a few days later. I regret I was not able to be there and only managed a brief return visit to Queenstown for his funeral.

Our jam business had grown significantly during this year, and Owen was becoming very busy with the farm work, jam sales, and compliance requirements. He needed me to assist with our own emerging business. I resigned, feeling satisfied at having accomplished the task I set out to do, the establishment of the school and government registration, which made it easy for the board to appoint a new teacher.

Unfortunately, by Easter 1991 with class numbers as high as seventeen, the newly appointed sole charge teacher found the class too difficult to handle and walked off the job. I received an emergency phone call asking me to come in, settle the upset children, and replace the teacher for the rest of the day. That request turned out to be the rest of the term!

It was great to be back with the children again, but my obligations at home did not allow me to make a full-time commitment, and so I found a wonderful teacher, Kathy King, to release me for four days a week. This worked for the rest of the year until another full-time teacher was appointed the following year.

After the new teacher had settled comfortably into the job, life at the school took a bad turn. The church began an outreach programme to the poor, and parents became upset when the children had to share the ablution block and grounds with all manner of people, including those with damaging addictions. When Owen and I heard of the parents' concerns, we approached the board, who explained to us that it was the high cost of the fees that had caused the withdrawal of their children. When we consulted with the parents, they told us quite a different story. They were concerned about the unsafe environment.

At this time, the government was mainstreaming disabled children from the Maitai School. After making enquiries, Owen and I discovered that it would be possible to share their buildings. The school was situated near our present premises with wonderful grounds and facilities, a science room, a library, a cooking room, and a gymnasium.

Owen and I made an appointment with the school principal. It was our good fortune that the morning we arrived for our appointment, the principal had received a letter from the education board informing her that rooms within her school could be leased to appropriate, compatible organizations. She accepted the idea of us leasing classrooms with enthusiasm and gave us a tour of the buildings and facilities available. We were thrilled and made arrangements with board members and parents to visit the school to discuss the arrangements. It was a wonderful opportunity to grow the school and enjoy all the facilities offered. The parents saw this as a perfect plan for the growth of the school, and they were happy to share the facilities with the children still to be schooled on the site. Two classrooms were offered to us.

Alas, the newly appointed teacher at the school did not agree with the new venue, claiming the classrooms were too small. The board of governors had no choice but to support their new teacher in this, and it was agreed between them that it was not the right solution.

Owen and I, along with the pupils' parents, had a vision for the school, but with opposition from the new teacher and the board of governors, it would prove unworkable. We knew we had been given a wonderful opportunity, but without vision and enthusiastic people, a dream will die. Owen and I retreated to our busy life on the farm.

Perhaps the board and the teacher were right, but the numbers dwindled, and the children left and enrolled in other schools. The All Saints School closed a short time later.

Pre-Supermarket Stocking

The growth of the jam market became our focus. We were a start-up business with limited finance, so we used the cheapest means possible to expand our business, which meant we were always hands-on with the potential markets and initial contacts.

To increase sales and expand our customer base, Owen and I spent the year travelling to the Christchurch Saturday Art Market, while our daughter, Shelley, who had left the bank to join us in the business, continued selling at the Nelson Market. Owen drove sales when he had the capacity to fill orders and no new outlets were opened up, until he knew he could continuously provide stock.

After a few months of selling our raspberry jam at the Christchurch Market, we figured that we had enough regular customers willing to shop in the local supermarkets for Owen to approach their buyers. In preparation for the next step, Owen sent two boxes of raspberry jam to the

Christchurch head office of Countdown Supermarkets, confident that he would not be turned away. However, it was not until after our visit to the regional stores around the South Island the following year that we put enough pressure on Countdown's head office to compel them to trial our raspberry jam in two of their Countdown Christchurch supermarkets.

Supermarket Culture

There were three major players in the New Zealand supermarket industry at this time. Woolworths, Progressive Enterprise, and Foodstuffs. Foodstuffs was a 100 per cent Kiwi owned and operated company with their regional groups, Auckland, Wellington Christchurch, and Dunedin.

In the 1990s, Foodstuffs supermarkets were privately owned and operated, and therefore they were easier to approach with new products. With the jam sales in the existing outlets of small shops increasing, Owen decided to present to Foodstuffs South Island. He sent off the brief presentation with the pricing and a carton of product.

The buyer at Foodstuffs loved the jam and agreed to host support it. This was our opportunity to prove that the jam would sell, because if it did not move off the shelf of the supermarket within a short period, it faced deletion. Hopefully we had enough existing customers for the jam to sell, although Owen was not quite sure – just as he wasn't sure what host supporting meant, but he did know that it guaranteed payment. As we visited individual supermarkets, we discovered that Foodstuffs' head office set prices and sent out shelf tickets to each store. We invoiced the head office, and they collected payment from each supermarket and paid us once a month.

Foodstuffs' normal mark-up for new lines like ours was 18 per cent. Because the supermarket was looking at the amount of money they make per square metre of shelf space, with good volume sellers like soft drinks, their margins did not need to be so high. When our jam became a high-volume seller, the margins dropped enormously. The costs of operating a supermarket retail outlet is dependent on many different things, but the return per square metre is a good indication of profitability. If those wishing to supply supermarkets understood this when approaching them, they would know whether they are likely to get their product stocked. A good way of doing this is to build a sales record through a local market, such as we did.

Owen had faith in his product, and he had already proved that there was a good profit margin in it for the shops. He bought a Ford trader truck that had been running up and down the Nelson wharf, and off we went on a tour around the South Island, loaded up with jam to present samples to the independently owned Foodstuffs supermarkets.

The owners and grocery buyers responded favourably to the good gross margins on the product, and they were impressed with our sales record. They liked the taste of the raspberry jam and the idea of farmer manufacturers. Owen displayed confidence in the quality of his product on our visits, and he worked hard at building a rapport with the buyers, owners, manager, and staff alike. He communicated his ideas with passion, never missing an opportunity to talk and share his stories. He disclosed sales figures, which included mail orders, proving the customer demand for our jam in their area. He then followed up with the question that he was always ready to ask: 'What can I do to get my jam into your supermarket?'

Sometimes the needs were reassurance that his product would sell, the profit margin, the competition for shelf space, continuity of supply, or some sympathy for a stressed-out buyer. Owen had answers and reassurances ready for each point raised, and the most effective way of answering their concerns was for them to raise them. Sometimes if that didn't happen, Owen would encourage them to share their concerns by asking again, 'What is it that I can do to help you put this product into your supermarket?'

Even at this early stage of the business, Owen's highest value was relationships. He prioritized it and walked it out, and his practices were governed by it. Developing this as a measure by which to govern his behaviour was not easy and took time, but it became a decision of the will, which was logical, and he found that it brought freedom. It became for him the life blood of the business. Today, it is still his highest value – relationships with the customers, supermarkets, staff, and family. Anyone who takes an interest in him and shares this value will find he has the time to talk, listen, and be interested.

I recall one experience we had. Owen approached a supermarket buyer that would have sent the bravest of fellow scurrying for cover, but not Owen. He stood his ground. On entering the supermarket, he introduced himself and asked the girl at the checkout if he could see the grocery buyer, which was his normal routine. She called for the man on the intercom, and the buyer sent a message back to say that he was unavailable.

Knowing that the supermarket was privately owned and the owner would be impressed when a manufacturer came knocking on his door, Owen asked the girl if they could see the owner of the supermarket. The girl called back to the grocery buyer, relaying Owen's request. The buyer quickly stormed out from his office at the back of the store, intent on confronting the intruder. Owen was waiting with a welcoming smile. As the buyer reached the entrance to the check out, he paused to yell across the counter at Owen, waiting patiently and composed on the other side. 'Well, what's your problem?'

Owen replied, 'You are. I'm trying to get my jam into your supermarket.'

Upon hearing, Owen's response, the guy lightened up, walked through the checkout, and listened to Owen's presentation. Somewhere along the line, it must have soothed his disposition. It was not long before he was purchasing two cartons of raspberry jam to stock in the store.

Owen was at his best standing in the face of rejection; he never became personally offended. He understood how dealing with the stress of every man and his dog, thinking they have the most wonderful product if only they could get it into the supermarket, could cause a strong reaction. Keeping the focus on the problem and off himself always helps in these situations.

On future visits to that store, this particular gentleman made the time to say hello, and he treated us like royalty when his sales quickly went from two boxes of jam to a pallet of eighty boxes every four weeks.

During this trip around the South Island visiting the Foodstuffs supermarkets, Owen decided it would be expedient for him to call on the managers of the Countdown supermarkets at the same time. Their head office in Christchurch was still going through the process of deciding whether or not they would stock the jam. If they did decide to stock it, Owen reasoned, he would have to make the same trip again to introduce it to these shops. With that in mind, and because he had not received any feedback from Countdown head office, he decided to include visits to their supermarkets on this tour.

He called on the Countdown supermarkets and gave their managers a sample of the product. The jam was well received in all their stores. The managers in the Countdown stores unbeknown to us, were so enthusiastic about it that they rang through to their head office and asked if and when they could begin stocking.

While heading back up to Christchurch, Shelley, our daughter who was running the office on the farm in Upper Moutere, telephoned us with the news that a very angry-sounding Tim Hamilton, from Countdown, wanted to see us in his Christchurch office as soon as possible. Later that week, when Owen and I arrived at Tim's office, he was very upset with us.

'I don't want the supermarket managers ringing me up and telling me what they are going to stock. I'll decide what goes into the supermarkets,' he stated furiously. Owen apologized profusely and said he did not know it was not the right way to do things. Then Tim went on to say, 'I don't know why I am doing this, Owen, with only one product and all the paperwork involved, but we will trial your raspberry jam in two stores for you, Northlands and South City.'

This was the break Owen wanted. He was convinced that once it went into the stores, customer demand would not permit it to be taken out. And that's exactly what happened!

Once the jam went into the supermarkets, we were required to service the store with regular visits to deliver product and ensure they carried enough stock until we called again. Our representative was also required to deal with damage stock and check shelf stock for cleanliness and rotation.

Supermarket Deliveries

Supermarket chains have their own distribution warehouses, where suppliers send pallets of goods which are then sent out to the supermarkets on a daily basis. A newcomer to the market, such as we were, needed to deliver directly into the supermarket and keep the shelf stocked. Empty shelves are not popular with supermarkets, because no stock on the shelf means no sales and no income on that shelf space. Owen employed his older brother, Ian, who was not working at the time, to call on the supermarkets fortnightly, check the shelves, and make deliveries from the stock he carried on the truck. Although we encouraged buyers to fax their orders through to the office, they sometimes failed to do so, or they under ordered. Ian would travel up to Nelson one week, pick up the jam and faxed orders from the farm, and then visit the supermarkets to check and replenish their stocks. It was a two-week cycle, Christchurch to Nelson one week, and Christchurch to Invercargill the second week, with the caravan in tow for accommodation. Ian commenced this visiting cycle after our introductory trip around the South Island.

On his first trip back from Invercargill, north of Balclutha, we received word that he had hit a sheet of black ice, rolled the truck (fortunately without the caravan in tow), and ended up in Dunedin Hospital. My mother was living with us at the time and could not be left alone, so Owen made the journey by himself. He drove twelve hours in our Mitsubishi Ute, through the night, to reach the hospital, where he was relieved to discover Ian had suffered no major injuries and was ready to check out. Owen immediately sprung into retrieval mode, and they drove south to the site of the accident, where the truck, was miraculously still on the side of the road. They unloaded the contents onto the Ute and arranged for the truck to be transported back to Nelson for repairs. Then after picking up the caravan in Dunedin and dropping Ian off in Christchurch, Owen arrived home to the Moutere some twenty-five hours later, fatigued and shattered from the experience. With the truck back on the road and Ian in good health the following week, we continued with the delivery plan.

Three years of travelling up and down the South Island delivering jam to the supermarkets increased sales considerably, and Owen received a phone call from the buyer of Foodstuffs' head office, Phil Lemon. Phil said, 'Owen, I have never done this before, and I am not likely to do it again. I have queues of people waiting for appointment times to see me, to tell me what amazing products they have, if I would only put it on the supermarket shelf. But here I am asking if we can stock your raspberry jam in our distribution warehouse.'

Owen was running short of raspberries for the jam, and he knew that by stocking in the warehouse, extra stock would be required. He was always honest in his dealings, so he regretfully replied, 'I'm sorry, Phil, but I can't do it yet. I need to wait until the new season's raspberries come in. Only then will we have enough stock to put in your warehouse.'

That was what happened the following year. When a product generates a large volume of sales, like our Anathoth Raspberry Jam was doing, it became compulsory for its supermarket members to stock, and it was worthwhile for it to be stored in distribution warehouses, where the company received its percentage. Being warehoused is an enormous advantage for any supplier, and its availability generates good sales, but for us it was exceptionally cost effective being a backload to two-thirds of the country from our district, resulting in greatly reduced transport costs. Now the supermarkets would do their own ordering of jam from the Foodstuffs warehouse every day.

Eventually we exchanged the Ford Trader for a new Ford Transit, for the dual purpose of carting pallets of jam into Nelson and returning with pallets of sugar. Then our caravan went over the strait and north to Otaki, parked on Stanmore's farm, and was used for accommodation on our promotional trips around the lower North Island.

Supermarket Servicing

When the supermarkets commenced ordering daily from their distribution centre, we needed to continue maintaining a presence in the stores by employing merchandisers. Ian continued as a merchandiser in the Christchurch area for a time, and we employed others to service the southern end of the island. We reviewed the merchandisers' weekly reports and took appropriate action when necessary.

It was still possible for Owen and me to continue paying regular visits to the supermarkets to discuss and give ongoing support to buyers, because the supermarket was our link to the end user and kept the wheels of sales turning. Like Ian when he was delivering jam, we would park our caravan in the supermarket car parks overnight and be woken by the milkman and the bread deliveries arriving in the early hours of the morning. Years later, people would affectionately bring up in conversation how they had seen our caravan and truck parked in the supermarket car parks.

These courtesy visits allowed us to track our sales and maintain approachable relationships with buyers, whom we relied on to give us good shelf space. Shelf position is important and reflects product sales. When we first entered the supermarkets, the spreads category was shrinking, and buyers became aware that our product was expanding the category. Because of this, we were guaranteed a good position on the shelf with plenty of shelf space.

Our jam was placed fifteen degrees below eye level, which is recognized as the most conspicuous height for display and generating higher sales. Being positioned on the bottom or top shelf yields less sales for the same product. Not cooperating with the supermarkets or not spending enough on promotions also determines shelf position, which could be taken by another supplier who is spending more. We had the experience of being repositioned to the bottom shelf once, when a new category manager for Progressive decided that he wanted us to pay more cooperative fees than the business could afford. Fortunately, the 'punishment' did not last long because the opposition received the benefit of increased sales of our jam.

It was a challenge launching a new grocery product, but we had wonderful support from the supermarket chains, and being able to use their warehousing and distribution channels made it so much easier. We learnt that establishing relationships with buyers, agents, and carriers were things that took time.

With successful supermarket sales, our jam production was doubling every year. We had gone from freezing five tons of raspberries to ten tons, and now twenty tones of raspberries went into the freezer, ready to turn into jam. Around this time, Owen decided to approach the New Zealand Sugar Company to negotiate a reasonable contract price for their sugar. He thought that if we could combine our sugar order with Herman Seifried, a wine grower in our valley, we would be a worthwhile customer. It was not to be. Owen was, told that he was a nuisance, and his custom would not be considered.

We did find a very good opposition company called Kerry New Zealand Ltd., importers of bulk sugar. We were able to begin buying our sugar with them on the futures market. A futures market is a central financial exchange where people can trade standardized futures contracts – that is, a contract to buy specific quantities of a commodity at a specified price with delivery set at a specified time in the future. The company representatives gave us exceptional service by advising us when to buy at the cheapest possible price. Owen would calculate how much sugar he required for the year and buy on the futures market, where it gave us the opportunity to buy sugar at a cheaper price.

When the NZ Sugar Company approached us in 2003 for business, their representative was informed of the way his company had dealt with us in the past. We received an apology from the general manager for their past behaviour towards us!

DSIR Jam Trial

In 1993, Harvey Hall from the Department of Scientific Industrial Research (DSIR) asked Owen and me to cook up thirty-five different varieties of raspberries in order to discover which variety of raspberries made the best jam. After we had cooked up the different varieties of jam from yellow berries, black berries, red berries and a mixture of summer and autumn berries, Harvey took the many different jars of jam to the New Zealand Agriculture Field Days in Hamilton.

The results were very conclusive. Eighty per cent of people who did the taste test preferred the jam made with our Marcy raspberries. This confirmed what Owen already knew: the raspberries that we grew on our farm in the Moutere clay had a high acid level and made the tastiest jam. Was it the land, or was it the way Owen managed and improved the land, or was it the whole art of farming husbandry that he implemented that made our berries so great?

Marcy raspberries used to be the most common variety of raspberries grown in New Zealand. They are high yielding and produce soft fruit with good flavour and colour, which make them very suitable for processing. However, they have become unpopular with growers because they are less suitable for machine harvesting.

Purposeful Building

Towards the end of 1993, Owen approached the ASB to inquire about the possibility of building accommodation for raspberry pickers. It was always an advantage to have a team of about sixty pickers on site, and we had been accommodating them in our house or in tents, as some preferred, which put pressure on our washing facilities. Our vision was to build a dual-purpose facility to house raspberry pickers during the season and an off-season ministry school run by Vineyard USA, with whom Owen had kept in touch. A regular income from the Nelson Market, along with a cash return for fresh raspberries and the sales of raspberry jam through the supermarkets, had our overdraft being peeled back, and future earnings looked assured. Therefore when Owen had plans drawn up for the proposed building, the bank had no objection to his request for finance.

Five cabins with enough room for two sets of bunks and a chest of drawers were in the plan. Then we planned a larger building with a big lounge and access to a small kitchen, together with three toilets and showers and a small laundry, made accessible from both sides of the building. Added to this was an outside covered patio with table and chairs for outside dining and smokers. The site was later landscaped with trees and shrubs, which created a pleasant garden environment.

At the same time Owen was planning to house workers, I requested a small alteration in the dining room of our house – perhaps a ranch slider that would give better inside access, rather than everyone filing through my small kitchen. However, Owen employed John White, a young architect from Ian Jack's office, to draw up plans for renovations that would take place over the next ten years. Owen's vision was for a large house that would provide enough living area to service and meet the needs of people drawn to buying a lifestyle block.

When the plans came back, we were thrilled and amazed at what had been accomplished. Our banana-shaped house, drawn on paper, had turned into something from the pages of a glossy magazine. The angles, extensions, and shapes of the rooms were practical and appealing. Now we had something to work towards in stages. The first stage began when a builder friend turned our pantry off the bedroom into an en-suite. I can still recall that feeling of luxury at having a bathroom all to ourselves, instead of sharing it with numerous backpackers.

With our budget and accounts submitted to the bank a year later, the finances became available to proceed with the planned construction of accommodation block and alterations to the house. The builders completed both jobs before the following raspberry season in December 1994.

Anaheim Vineyard Family

Early in 1994, Owen fulfilled his long-cherished dream: a visit to John Wimber's church in Anaheim, California. His desire was to experience first-hand church members 'doing the stuff'.

In preparation for the visit, Owen rang the church office to ask if there was a place to stay while visiting. We were thrilled when we were told that Dennis and Cynthia Riggs would be more than happy to be our hosts. Owen began communicating with Cynthia and planned to stay with them for a week. Then while attending a conference at the church, we would stay at the Holiday Inn, after which we had another five weeks in Anaheim but no planned accommodations.

We stepped off the plane and got a rental car, ready to drive down the freeway on the 'wrong' side of the road to Anaheim, which was about an hour south of Los Angeles. I thought Owen was so courageous!

By mistake, we turned off the freeway too soon. Deciding we were quite lost, we pulled up at a small garage to ask for directions. From my seat in the car, I watched nervously as Owen pulled out a hundred-dollar bill and went into the garage to get change for the telephone box outside in the car park, to ring Cynthia. Our surroundings were urban and had a slum-like appearance marked by run-down housing and poverty – a place where you would likely be mugged for a lot less than a hundred dollars!

After managing to change the money unscathed, Owen put a call through to Cynthia. After a few exchanges with Cynthia, she asked, 'Where are you?' On hearing Owen's reply to her question, she went quiet. Then after giving him clear directions about how to get back on the freeway, she commanded him to get straight back in the car and drive out of there immediately. She told us later that the area was like the Bermuda Triangle, where people disappeared!

We followed Cynthia's directions and navigated our way safely to the Riggs's luxurious home in the Anaheim Hills, where we received a warm welcome from Cynthia and Dennis. Dennis was a veterinarian with a clinic in the Anaheim Shopping Centre, where Cynthia also worked some days. Owen offered to pay his way, but Dennis declined his offer, saying that we were his guests for the week.

The raspberry jam we'd brought over from New Zealand was very much enjoyed, and it was served up on their dinner plate. Jam and meat?

We spent the week getting to know the Riggs and their friends, and finding our way about Anaheim. Then we left them to stay at the Holiday Inn during the conference. However, after the conference, they were kind enough to invite us back to their home to complete the remaining weeks of our holiday.

Doing the Stuff

We found the Vineyard church sited in an industrial complex in Anaheim. The building was large enough to house a school, along with numerous administration and meeting rooms and a large auditorium that could seat about five thousand people. The same area was repeated upstairs. The building was enormous and provided wonderful facilities, and the grounds surrounding it were plentiful and large enough for more than a couple of rugby games.

Upon entering the building, this enormous, life-size bronze sculpture of Jesus washing Peter's feet, depicting Christ's servanthood, dominated the foyer, forging such an emotional connection that one could not fail to grasp the values of the church.

As we moved on through to the main auditorium, the first thing that drew our attention was a spectacular banner that affirmed and proclaimed another Vineyard value: 'Mercy Triumphs over Judgment' was suspended over the stage. The seating in the auditorium was arranged in sloping tiers, and there were many rooms leading off into other areas. It was an awesome building inside and out, and it became our home on Sundays as we participated in all the activities they had to offer. We received a warm welcome when we attended early Sunday morning classes, and we were offered a choice of eight classes dealing with different issues, all led by church staff. After classes, we attended the morning service at 10.00 a.m., where outside the west tunnel leading into the auditorium we came upon 'Newcomers Connection' booths, where information on services and how to be connected with Vineyard Anaheim were available.

We joined Dennis and Cynthia in the auditorium, where people in casual dress flowed in, ready for the worship to begin. In some congregations, worship is often used as a warm-up for the teaching, but not here. This congregation addressed God directly in song, giving Him worship as a gift, and then they followed the presence of God as he ministered to them. The Vineyard are known for their music and have invested in quality musicianship and technology. They birthed a special music ministry with a recording and distribution company, Vineyard Music, which Owen had joined some years before. The short teaching time in the service was followed by a time of ministry, and Owen was always ready and willing to get his share.

After service every Sunday, the church fed about a thousand people at a Lamb's Lunch, and we joined the volunteers to help. When people arrived, they were given a paper bag lunch, and the worship team sang while they ate. A Vineyard member shared his or her testimony and followed up with an offer to pray for anyone in need. Many came forward.

As the people left, they were, given a large paper bag full of groceries to feed them for the week. Attached to this ministry was a budget for clothes and a ministry to the prisons. When prisoners came out, they were issued with a suitcase of clothes of their choice and a bus ticket to their preferred destination. The Spanish Service followed the Lamb's Lunch. The service was all in Spanish, but we were lucky enough to have an interpreter, someone who wanted to practice his English. Then each Sunday we would finish our busy day with the six o'clock evening service.

Staying with Dennis and Cynthia was like being in the heart of Vineyard, with home group meetings and friends who came to their house during the week specifically to pray for us.

We had arrived in Anaheim on January 20, 1994, three days after the 6.7 magnitude earthquake had struck in Reseda, the north-central San Fernando Valley region, thirty-one kilometres northwest of downtown Los Angeles. We were invited to go along on an outreach to the people most affected by the earthquake, a migrant community with many residents made homeless and unable to access welfare. The Anaheim Vineyard had the resources and were able to send doctors, nurses, dentists, and other professional personal to support the local Vineyard fellowship. The volunteers assisting with the ministry carpooled up to the area and spent time in worship before the journey and after we arrived. Three trucks were loaded with food, medicines, and musical equipment and were taken into the area.

In a supermarket car park, the area was transformed! The musicians were set up on a stage in the centre of the car park, with tables and chairs ready for the residents surrounding them in café style. Numerous tents erected down one side of the car park were screened off as booths. Behind the screens, doctors, nurses, and other health workers prepared for health checks, and other booths were set aside for prayer.

After the setup was completed, many teams made up of five or six people went out in search of residents to invite them back to the car park and receive all that was offered. We found people sleeping and cooking over open fires outside in the courtyards of the two-storey, shabby, and neglected accommodation blocks; they were too scared to venture inside. Many residents traumatized by the earthquake and aftershocks willingly came to receive practical and spiritual comfort. The outreach in the Reseda Valley was a demonstration of the genuine compassion and care Vineyard ministered, and it left a lasting impression on all who took part.

While we were in Anaheim, Owen had planned a drive up to San Luis Obispo, 346 kilometres north of Los Angeles, to meet with Bob Crane, an itinerant Vineyard pastor who led the San Luis Obispo Vineyard. We had met Bob at a conference in New Zealand, and he had expressed an interest in teaching at our proposed ministry school.

We caught up with Bob at his office and, after a preparatory discussion, agreed to keep in touch. Bob's assistant later wrote to Owen concerning the School of Ministry, saying Bob wanted to commence in March 1995. They corresponded in detail the sleeping arrangements required for the students, and their needs for an ablution block and cooking facilities. Then he discussed advertising, pricing of the school, and numbers to attend. Regrettably, the school never commenced because Bob's circumstances changed, but we went ahead and built the accommodations anyway.

While in Anaheim, we were excited to find and visit a Trader Joe shop. Trader Joe stores are throughout America and stock great tasting food. A New Zealand sales agent had submitted our jams to Trader Joes head office so we decided to ask how far we were through the submission process. When we called into their head office here, they said there was only one stage to go through, and that was the taste test. We thought we were home and hosed because the taste of the product was our best attribute and the major selling point. They were going to let us know the outcome within a week. We haven't heard from them since!

Leaving Anaheim after eight weeks of enjoyable company from like-minded people and experiencing all that Vineyard had to offer, especially the kindness and fellowship, triggered a flood of tears from Owen as he boarded the plane. I was nostalgic and keen to return home.

Seasonal Workers

By 1994 the raspberry growers in the district, including us, were struggling to find pickers for the upcoming raspberry harvest. Every year, it was the same story. Our large crop, combined with new plantings coming into production this year, had Owen concerned that we would not have enough pickers for the harvest. In preparation for the season, Owen gauged the number of employees required by growers for the berry harvest and discovered that approximately seven hundred workers were needed. He also predicted that there were not enough students seeking summer work or locals to fill the vacancies. Knowing that a labour shortage would affect not only the income of our local growers but also the export market, he went to the Department of Labour with his concerns. Owen's solution to the labour shortage was to employ more backpackers, and he was hopeful that the Immigration Department would allow berry growers to increase the number of work visas for our area. With the high number of sunshine hours, bush tracks, rivers, and beaches to enjoy, we could attract many backpackers; Nelson was the ideal place to do seasonal work.

The department refused to issue visas and decided they could supply the grower's needs with local labour.

To achieve this, all unemployment benefits were cut off, and the beneficiaries were sent to the berry gardens around the district for growers to deal with! Because we now had accommodations and Nelson was a favourite holiday destination, we became inundated with young unemployed people sent by the Department of Labour from all around the country. Many needed to be cared for because they arrived without food or money and with numerous emotional problems. It proved very difficult to gain their attendance in the field each day, let alone pick raspberries.

Then they complained to the Labour Department about their pay! The department challenged Owen about workers not making the minimum wage. In retaliation, Owen stood up in the presence of the officers and mimed the action of picking a berry. He picked a berry and counted out loud one second, two seconds, three seconds, and demonstrated that in that time he could turn around, gaze at the sky for a time, scratch his bum and drop the berry into the bucket before turning back to the bush. This exercise demonstrated that pickers only had to pick a berry every three seconds to make the minimum wage.

The department was satisfied and had to agree that the unemployed people were not focused. In their defence, however, just as milking a cow by hand is a learnt skill, so is harvesting berries from the bush. The best pickers were fourteen-year-olds motivated to earn money.

Owen set up supervisors in the field, one for every twenty workers, to deal with the inexperienced raspberry pickers. Supervisors trained workers in the art of picking and ensured that pickers had the proper equipment, white liver pails that sat in a frame and fitted into a belt around their waists.

They checked the buckets for leaves and twigs, and they ensured that rows were picked cleanly; berries left on the vine go mouldy when it rains and spoil any new fruit. Supervisors also assisted pickers to stay on the job, and have sun protection and appropriate clothing.

Owen was patient in dealing with difficult behaviour in the field. After tearing the fruit off the vines, one chap came to the sorting shed and dumped the bucket under Owen's nose, saying 'How's this, then?'

Obviously he wanted to be fired, but instead Owen did not let the chap get the better of him. Owen quietly replied, 'You need to go back to the supervisor, and he will show you again how to pick the fruit.'

Not getting the response he was looking for, the guy swore disgustingly and headed for the gate.

Many unemployed came and went just as quickly during the season, causing much wasted time in training, filing paperwork, and signing in and out. Little wonder that berry farmers began to look elsewhere for assistance in harvesting their crops.

Machine Harvesting

As the country's leadership moved the responsibility for maintaining an efficient and motivated work force to the employer and completely exempted workers from their responsibility to perform, it became apparent to growers that hand-picking berries would become problematic. This situation, would now affect the harvesting of our crops. There were very few skilled harvesters left now that could make a reasonable income. Now growers were legally required to provide that income, whether or not the pickers performed well. Before the1994–1995 raspberry season, our neighbour purchased a new Korvan harvester and asked Owen to trial it on our berries. Owen agreed. The picking machine arrived from America before the raspberry season with the sales manager for Korvan, who stayed with us for the week to trial the machine. Every day the American was in the field to demonstrate and give instruction to the driver on the use of the harvester. Machine harvesting raspberries often produces lower yields than hand picking, and sadly, this was the case with our Marcy berries. The projected fifty-ton crop fell to twenty-three tons. Initially our jam was sold at around the same price as other jams, but when we had our poor harvest, Owen knew that we needed an income to survive until the next year's harvest. He increased the price of our jam by fifty cents and hoped to slow down sales.

However, our raspberry jam kept outselling all other raspberry jams in the supermarkets, where it had been stocked for twelve months or more. In some cases, it was selling double that of its nearest rival. In order to cover the shortfall, we were obliged to buy raspberries from other growers. The concerns about harvesting and the Department of Labour's continual harassment caused Owen to disregard the poor performance of the small machine and import a more sophisticated Korvan 9000, which was a self-propelled, over-the-row harvester, with the expectation that it would pick more efficiently.

The garden was very quiet without the hundred or so pickers moving around, and the birds feasting undisturbed became a serious problem. Although he tried very hard to pick with the machine. the berries still did not come off easily. It became more efficient to return to hand picking and use the machine when the pickers could not keep up with a flush in the crop, or when they refused to work on the day before Christmas.

Owen was always interested in the natural propagation of raspberries plants from bird droppings or plants interbreeding, and he was quick to distinguish new varieties in our garden. The new variety of a raspberry plant, called Moutere, came from a plant that Owen identified in our raspberry garden as bearing berries with a weight of up to five grams early in the season. He saw the fruit as excellent punnet berries, so he gave the plant to the DSIR to have propagated. When the plants were ready, Owen purchased enough to plant out a row in our garden. Then when showing people around the farm, he would say proudly, 'They are my experimental raspberries.' The new raspberry plant was aptly called Moutere and is available in nurseries around the country today. It sells as far afield as Australia.

Nelson Business Award

In 1995 a Chamber of Commerce member, Judy Finn, invited Owen to enter the Tasman Energy Small Business Awards. Owen was fortunate enough to win. He was modest about his success because as he said, all he had done was grow some raspberries, cooked them up into jam, and put the jam on supermarket shelves, where it sold because of its popularity. The sales value in raspberry jam had shown a significant increase each year.

- 1992–93: $122,724
- 1993–94: $191,586
- 1994–95: $244,509

There had been no great scientific or technical development utilized to produce this product, and neither had there been any tantalizing or tempting promotional programme to entice people into buying the jam. There was a high customer demand for the product and an excellent mark-up of 18 per cent for the retailer.

The following year, when Owen was asked about the advantages gained from the honour of winning the award, he responded by saying, Identifying specific benefits to our business from entering and being successful in the Small Business Award was a difficult exercise. There were so many factors contributing to the success of our business that it is difficult to view one aspect of the business, outside of a relationship to everything else that is going on. Our sales for 1993 had increased by 31 per cent on the previous year; this would make the most solemn person crease into a small smile. So it was with some hilarity that we welcomed a further increase of 100 per cent in sales this year, and our feelings are bordering on terror, at our budgeted 100 per cent increase for the next financial year. Only yesterday we noticed an increase in local sales as a direct result of the brief mention we received on the local radio. After winning the award, we made the front page of the *Guardian*, a full-page feature in the February issue of *Horticulture News*, and a special mention by Elisabeth Pedersen in her food column in the *New Zealand Herald*.

It would cost a small fortune to buy that sort of advertising in the newspaper. Commerce Nelson is doing an outstanding job supporting Nelson businesses, and in particular the Business Awards that give people like us recognition for the many years of effort necessary to establish a new business. My only regret is that I am unable to participate in more of the Chamber's activities, but as you can probably guess, Kaye and I are having a little difficulty in finding enough time to sleep.

All our success had come about with our one and only product at this time: raspberry jam. Our packaging continued to be very simple: plastic pottles with not much in the way of labelling.

After the success in the Business Awards, the next stage of the business was upon us. The supermarkets and customers asked us to increase our range of products. It was there for the taking, and if we didn't do it, someone else would!

An Approach from Growers

In 1995 a blackberry grower contacted Owen and asked if he would consider buying his blackberries for jam. Owen told him that he was a farmer and didn't really want to be a manufacturer, but he would support him in making blackberry jam and market it alongside our raspberry jam. When the grower agreed to Owen's proposal, he came with his wife to our factory and perfected Owen's system of jam making. We then supported and mentored him into manufacturing. Although that grower, who also grew tomatoes, later pulled out, it did birth the idea of growers manufacturing their own products. We continued producing blackberry jam until another blackberry grower joined us.

When a magazine article was written about us, Owen took the opportunity in the article to invite other farmers growing fruit to establish factories for jam making on their farms. The first to respond was the blackberry grower from Te Horo. The farmer came to our factory and videoed our operation, and then he entered into agreements with us to set up and register a commercial kitchen. In no time he was making the blackberry jam.

A strawberry farmer from Waimate was next to approach us. He initially wanted to sell two tons of last year's strawberries, but we were ready to proposition him about manufacturing his strawberries into jam. His farm already made small quantities of jam in their kitchen for a self-serve roadside fruit stall, but he was not confident about cooking strawberry jam. We worked with the farmers for a time, teaching them the recipe that would produce a strawberry jam that had consistency and flavour. However, after they had been manufacturing for a few months, Owen found that the quality and variety of their strawberries, along with their method of cooking, was not producing a consistent jam. Therefore with their agreement, he terminated their contract, and they happily continued making many different jams for their roadside stall and local markets. When the strawberry growers contract was cancelled, Te Horo took over supply of the strawberry jam and later added plums to their range.

A Blenheim apricot grower also responded to the article and telephoned, 'I'm your man.' The owner of a ten-hectare block of apricots on Jefferies Road, he was looking to diversify further when he read the article on our jam. He visited our factory with his wife, and two months later they were building a commercial kitchen to manufacture and process half a ton of apricot jam a day.

Cash flow can be a restraint on farming, as all farmers know, and the advantage of turning your crop into jam meant a welcomed regular monthly income. With farmer growers joining the team, the range of jams extended, and by 1997 we had added blackberry, strawberry, apricot, marmalade, plum, and boysenberry. The farmers were very enthusiastic about producing a good homemade product with high fruit content, and the regular income made their farms look very profitable. These small, team-based factory units, on farms with owner supervision and local labour, worked efficiently.

The following year, an approach came from someone with an interest in making boysenberry jam with the intention of planting the vines on their land. When they did not plant out boysenberries as agreed, Owen leased a boysenberry block to supply them, because our priority as farmers was to add value to what we grew. With the responses we had from growers, our lawyer was kept busy from April to September drafting up confidentiality and manufacturing agreements for our prospective factory owners. Although communicating our values and vision was difficult for farmers to grasp, we felt confident that when they saw the return received from adding value to their crops, they would become enthusiastic about the project.

From those early days, we knew and identified the essential elements that made our products so popular, and they were now being invited to piggy-backed on the success of our raspberry jam in the supermarkets. However, we did not take into account people's character, or their need to have personal recognition and ownership. Often recognition and making money, are the motivating forces behind what people want for themselves.

Over the years, as we spent time dealing with farmers, Owen discovered that farmers are very difficult people to deal with.

We also sold raspberry jam and raspberry vinegar at the market.

In the early days at the market, we met an Australian raspberry grower who gave us a recipe for raspberry vinegar.

Raspberry pies and raspberry vinegar were then added to our range and sold at the market.

PART 4

Anathoth Marketing (AML)

Our raspberry farming and jam manufacturing operated as a sole trader under a partnership, O. J. & K. L. Pope. When other farmers joined our supply chain, Owen knew that it would be prudent to add to our business structure a limited liability company, thereby redirecting the risk from us as individuals and on to the company. Because our jam carried the Anathoth logo, the name Anathoth Marketing Limited was chosen for our new company. With Owen and me as the only directors and shareholders, decisions were made quickly and easily. If products weren't selling, they were not manufactured. That way products were always kept fresh in flavour. In contrast to that, a business run by a board with numerous directors cannot turn the ship and change direction quickly or efficiently, so their products can be well aged before they hit the shelves.

The new incorporated company came into existence under the Companies Act of 1993 on 21 November 1996, and the partnership remained separate from the selling and distribution of the jams. Anathoth Marketing had legal confidentiality agreements and specifications for the products, and it took responsibility for all matters relating to marketing. The New Zealand Company Register records the original Anathoth Marketing Limited that Owen formed and the company names that followed. The company is identified by its allocated number, and therefore the history of the company can be lost when the name is changed, as it did in our case later when investors entered the company.

Anathoth Marketing Ltd began its life with our son, Tim, as manager. He had a BSc, a BA, and work experience including picking raspberries as a youth, working on our raspberry garden, supervising the harvests, and managing apple orchards.

Owen, as with all aspects of our business, was hands-on in establishing the marketing company's role and guiding the interaction and procedures to develop satisfying relationships with suppliers and customers alike. As with every facet of the business, he left his handprints all over it.

The fruit growers and factory owners worked under an exclusive contract, owning and operating their own factories. They were trained and given ongoing assistance in the use of Owen's original cooking system, as modelled in our factory. In order to produce the jams efficiently, Owen's system had to be strictly adhered to, because the wage content increases and the quality of a product decreases when employees make changes to the system. This is identified in manufacturing terms as creep.

Creep can occur when an employee changes one action, then another, and so on until you finally end up with inefficiencies and a very different product. There is a cost to picking up an item and putting it down without completing the purpose it was picked up for. It increases wages and employment, and in a free and competitive market, it is not sustainable. Owen continually reminded our employees that if you pick it up once, don't put it down until it's dealt with!

The new company was charged with developing distribution systems and filling orders. Our sales manager dealt with any complaints about products or services. All complaints were treated quickly and generously by staff, and Owen trained them to see the situations as an opportunity to build positive contact. The company monitored and checked manufacturing process and liaised with growers and manufacturers.

New products were developed by the marketing company. They predicted each farmer and manufacturer sales, and then they recorded, ordered, and paid for stock. Owen's intention was to return as much as possible to the farmers so that they could develop and invest in their farms.

Just as Owen's manufacturing process was unique, so was his approach to the production of raw product. The produce on the farms was grown purely for manufacture, and produce was harvested when the acid level was right for preserving. With inferior, second-grade fruit came an inferior, second-grade product. The factories manufacturing on the farms in Blenheim, Mahana, Otaki, and Waimate were easily supervised by owners. They also provided rural communities with employment.

Hands-on Directorship

Owen was readily available and a phone call away, governing like a pro with values, priorities, and beliefs from the heart, which weren't just whims but actual practices that facilitated decision making. Situations became less dramatic under his watch.

He saw every negative situation as an opportunity to turn it into a positive one. He was gifted with insight and came up with the solution to situations by thought without any real experience, sometimes quickly or at other times with well-thought-out reasoning; either way, he always knew how to move the business forward.

By never compromising his priorities of quality, service, efficiency, and profitability, he had the recipe for successful sales that made our fledgling business grow. Owen steered our business like the entrepreneur he is, a generator of new ideas and business processes with management skills and a strong team-building ability.

When he was planning, he never made decisions by looking at the competition and running with their whims, like a cat chasing its tail. If he did that, he concluded that they would be running his business, and he never liked anyone else calling the shots for him! He also thought differently than an accountant. He knew what his customers wanted and provided the goods and services to meet their needs, which in turn provided growth for the business. Accountants record the past transactions of a business to show its company's profitability, which is not the best practice to set its direction. Owen often said that if this is allowed to happen, it's like the accountant is sitting on the back of the Ute and looking at where you are happily travelling, and he will often reach through the window and try to steer the vehicle. Then inevitably when you come to the first corner, you run into the bank!

As our reputation for our raspberry jam grew, so also did our brand name Anathoth. It was an opportunity to communicate the Christian message and to tell the biblical story of Anathoth. People had difficulty pronouncing the name and would often say, 'The jam with the funny name.' Initially the supermarket buyers thought it was a Greek jam because of its name. The plastic pot and the brand name did their job because they were easily recognized when it came to a rebuy.

Owen loved the name even more as he saw the vision he had of the derelict, run-down raspberry farm being restored, as promised in Jeremiah 32. It was a name with deep meaning for Owen, and because it had become our trademark and brand, a unique identifier, he saw the need to register it with the Intellectual Property Office.

Owen and I had sacrificed much for our Anathoth brand, and it added value to our business in the form of goodwill because of it. The goodwill increased substantially over the next few years as the brand established itself throughout Australasia.

Moving with Technology

By June 1997, raspberry jam sales had gone from twelve and a half thousand pots to eighteen thousand pots a month. With all the added varieties of jams now in the supermarkets, Anathoth Marketing sales, along with our share of the jam category, had risen well past that number, and our five factories were set up with the capacity to produce even more, forty thousand pots each a month. It was time to expand our markets!

The business was taking off, and Owen was now dealing with technological changes and high-tech computer systems. He expanded the Reece accounting system to help organize the invoicing, accounts, and stock records. He employed a full-time accountant, plus an offsite accountant. Our cabins for accommodation became offices for five different managers, each furnished with the latest technology. Owen had engaged the Cawthron Institute in Nelson for product information and regular testing of the jams for shelf life, fermentation, and mould, and he continued the testing throughout the life of the business. Although he desired to set up a laboratory testing on the farm, we lacked the available expertise, and it never happened.

Over the next five years, we increased our jam sales and became high-volume sellers in the major supermarket chains in the South Island. It was only when Owen was confident that he could maintain a continuous supply to our existing markets that he made it available to the lower North Island, and he began supplying into the Wellington area. He approached Wellington Foodstuffs, who because of our sales record in the South Island agreed to host support us. When talking with the category buyer of Foodstuffs, Owen was ambitious and asked, 'What would happen if our brand became the market leader?'

The buyer's quick and insolent reply was, 'That will never happen.' His answer was like waving a red flag in front of a bull!

Owen said quietly to himself, 'Here is this smart-arse little prick with an inflated ego who is controlling the whole world, but there are two participants in this bull fight, and sometimes the bull wins!'

A product can become a market leader if sales increase above all other products in that category. If that happens, the supermarkets will drop their percentage back and sell the product below its minimum profit margin. It becomes what is known in the trade as a lost leader. Supermarkets use a lost leader to draw customers into their store, and the loss of profit is made up when other items are purchased.

We came to understand the impact of that while we were standing near the checkout with a supermarket owner one day. He said as he spied the baby food going over the counter, 'Well, there goes another cent!' This remark disclosed to us that it was a market leader.

Unbeknownst to me, way back in 1995, I did not understand that Owen envisioned being so successful that our product would become compulsory stocking and a lost leader. To earn this status in the supermarket chain as we did made our business very valuable indeed!

With the North Island market beginning to stock our jams, we then set out to visit individual supermarkets and promote our jam by giving away samples. We parked our caravan on Stanmore's Farm in Otaki, which we found was a convenient base to do promotional day trips. Then we travelled the lower half of the North Island from Wellington to Palmerston North, New Plymouth, Napier, Hastings, Masterton, and back with a carload of jam.

It was a vast area, but we covered it in two weeks and then followed up supermarket orders with postal deliveries from our farm, until enough supermarkets were stocking it. Then Foodstuffs Wellington took pallets into their distribution centre.

The arrival of our jam into their warehouse was announced to supermarkets via a fax, which told them that the very successful line of Anathoth Jams, sold throughout the South Island, was now available through Foodstuffs Wellington.

Servicing North Island Supermarkets

Although our jam was announced to the grocery buyers of Foodstuff's stores as arriving in their warehouse, it remained our job to persuade the individual stores to place an order and stock it. We travelled around the lower North Island introducing ourselves to the individual store buyers and giving away samples, after which we employed university students to do our follow-up servicing; some came to work on the farm for the raspberry harvest. With the increased number of merchandisers and growing sales administration, staff members were added to the team on the farm, as well as a sales manager, receptionist, and accounts person in the office. In the early days of our jam making, all our staff, be it office or factory workers, enjoyed working on the farm with Owen and I during the raspberry harvest. Now with the growth in jam sales and the need for continuity in administration, that option had passed.

Developing the North Island supermarkets came at a cost and was significantly subsidized by our sales in the South Island. We were reluctant to open up the Auckland market, but they were ready and waiting for us, and once again Foodstuffs Auckland co-supported us and announced our arrival to the supermarkets. Owen and I visited the supermarkets from Taupo in the South to Whakatane on the East Coast, and we went north as far as Whangarei, introducing ourselves to the buyers, giving out samples, and taking orders, which were then sent from the farm by courier. Then we spent six weeks living in our caravan at the Auckland Remuera Camping Grounds while pushing into the supermarkets. Our youngest son, Mark, had now joined the business and was working with us to deliver into the Auckland supermarkets using our delivery van. Raspberry, apricot, and marmalade had been ranged (which meant compulsory stocking) with the Foodstuffs group, but it still meant visiting the stores, talking to the buyer, and making regular deliveries to get it stocked on the shelf and keep it there. Some supermarkets took it on the first visit, and others required many return visits before it was accepted. Persuading the stores to take enough stock until the next two-weekly delivery became a problem because they had no sales history with which to gauge their reordering, so often the shelves would be empty before our return visit.

Owen remembers one bad trip when introducing the jam to a store while staying with his brother in Hamilton. I was confined to bed with a very bad dose of the flu, so that day Owen took his brother in my place on the supermarket visits. When they called at this particular supermarket, they were greeted with an angry owner, who accused Owen of sending a stupid fax announcing his visit; in fact, he said it was the stupidest fax he had ever received in his life. Owen wondered if the language might have been modified if I was present. Anyway, it took two years and a great deal of perseverance before that store put the jam on the shelf.

By May of that year, we were pushing into all the supermarkets in the North Island with a larger range of jams: raspberry, blackberry, apricot, strawberry, and marmalade. Owen and I did many tastings in numerous supermarket to promote our products, but then the area and number to reach became too numerous and widespread to service. Owen hired Professional Demonstration and Merchandising Ltd and initiated tastings in stores, and they reported back to us the many positive comments customers made. At one supermarket, a man approached the demonstrator. He didn't want to taste the jam. He said that there was no way he was going to get home unless he bought some raspberry jam, which his young son had tasted, gone out to the car, and ordered him to get some. He even told his dad where it was made and that it was natural.

Although we were stocked in many supermarkets in the Auckland area, it was still absent on the shelves of some stores, and we needed high sales or else ran the risked of being deleted. With low sales figures, products are always under threat of being deleted, and now it was serious business because we were responsible for the income of other farmers and many employees!

It is also a concern if the volume of sales isn't there because the marketing costs are high. The development of the North Island market was still being supported by the profits from an existing strong South Island market, so we continued to put a great deal of effort and money into getting this market up and running to support itself. One such store that had not stocked our product was the

Eastridge New World, the new flagship for Auckland Foodstuffs at that time, and an important store to stock. We tried to get the product stocked by talking to the young grocery buyer, but he was not willing to risk putting it on the shelf, as he said, 'On the off chance that it sells, and I will have to take something off the shelf to make room for it.' When Owen made every effort to reassure him that it sold well in the South Island, the man was quick to reply, 'South Islanders have different tastes.'

Blatantly exposing the rivalry that exists between the North and the South Islands, he had just stocked a French jam in a fancy glass bottle at the premium end of the jam market, and he saw ours as a lower price at the top end of the everyday jams. With our plastic pot and a higher price than the middle-ranged jams, we didn't fit the box into which the buyers always tried to put us. Faced with such resistance from the buyer at Eastridge New World, Owen and I knew that we had to generate customer demand for the product. We came up with a plan!

We walked around the residential area surrounding the supermarket, dropping off leaflets about ourselves and our jam. We took every opportunity to speak to people who were outside their homes, mowing lawns, or walking along the street. Our story was always the same: farmers growing fruit and making jam the old-fashioned way for a living, and trying to get the Eastridge supermarket to stock our jam.

People were very interested in our story, and once again our persistence paid off because within a few weeks, an order came for a pallet of jam from the Eastridge New World supermarket! Supermarkets thrive on customer demand. If it's what people want, supermarkets will give it to them!

Still more pushing into the Auckland market was required, so we advertised with Radio Rhema, and many listeners heard the advertisement. Then we did a major expensive advertising campaign with Radio New Zealand, which lasted six weeks. The radio station did a couple of skits and followed them up with a 'granny swap'. By bringing in a jar of homemade jam, it could be exchanged for a pot of Anathoth, and then all the jams brought in were donated to the City Mission outreach for the homeless. Again, for the Auckland area, we employed part-time merchandisers in each area to visit the supermarkets to stock, tidy shelves, and take orders. They were given a procedure sheet for the supermarkets, an hourly rate of pay, and training from us before being sent off.

The business was changing fast, and we had moved fairly rapidly from the start-up business of jam making through a growth and expansion period into supermarkets with immense success. With the skills Owen and I possessed and the help of staff, we had established a customer base, supermarket presence, and market acceptance of our products, and we had the experience and passion that was needed to drive the business forward, so along with the growth, Owen ensured that the structure and expanded business plan were there for the future.

The biggest challenge our growing company faced was dealing with the constant range of issues. Unpredictable circumstances – such as contract farmers wanting out of supplying or fruit shortages, especially for apricots and raspberries – affected our business model. When we could not grow or buy enough raspberries on the local market, we were forced to look at importing from America. Owen would ring up a contact in the United States and surprisingly not have to pay for the container loads until they arrived on the Nelson wharf, so trusting was the business climate of the 1990s.

We needed to train management staff and delegate responsibilities to move with this stage of growth. Family members had joined us: Shelley was factory manager, Timothy was in the marketing company, and Mark started in sales and then became farm manager. Added to that were store managers, production managers, accountants, and health and safety experts, and compliance programmes were kept up to date.

When away from the supermarkets and on his own turf, Owen was comfortable talking business around the kitchen table, whereas I was usually present in an informal manner. He was full of ideas and could talk nineteen to the dozen in an effort to convey his message, and many a meal was served over late-night discussions. Owen was good at finding knowledgeable people to complement his approach, and he did not hesitate to call on external assistance such as sales agents, because his focus was on quality, service, and efficiency to make better business practices.

Twin Agencies

Wayne Sands entered our lives when Owen and I were ready to shed the responsibility of supermarket merchandising and all its issues. We first met Wayne when he called at our stall in the Nelson market and identified himself as the owner of the marketing company Twin Agencies. He had a sales and merchandising service focused on caring for two New Zealand manufacturers Whittaker's Chocolates and Hubbard's Breakfast Food.

Many sales agents approached Owen in the past, asking to merchandise for him. When they offered to smarten up his label and change his packaging, Owen found it so offensive that his response was to send them packing with an equally negative message. Owen was an innovator, and his smartly designed plastic pot with its simple message communicated exactly what he wanted it to. Why would he want to change it? The plastic pot for jam was still a new concept and was developed in the 1980s. Changing the perception of jam from glass jars to plastic was difficult for some to accept, but our customers loved it!

Wayne Sands was the only sales agent who came to us saying, 'If it ain't broke, don't fix it.' He offered to provide the link between the manufacturer and retailer. Owen was so impressed with Wayne's values that he gave him a pot of jam and an invitation to call back. Our sales growth had spread throughout New Zealand, and we needed experienced personnel available to represent us in the supermarkets, so when Wayne responded to Owen's invitation to call at our home, he did just that and added us to his existing client base, saying, 'Love the brand and the product.'

Owen and I were delighted to shed the workload and pass the marketing of our products to Wayne. Like Owen, he focused on creating long-term relationships. His company had a reputation for providing exceptional service and quality products that built trust with customers, and those values fitted in with us like a hand in a glove! Wayne had divided New Zealand into special geographical areas serviced by area managers, who each had a team of merchandisers to visit and service the supermarkets. Their managers worked hard to find and secure an appropriate number of facings in the right spot for our products by liaising and pushing the product in the supermarkets – important for the continued growth of sales. At the request of the supermarket buyer, our agents would be permitted to do a jam relay, which happens when all the brands are taken from the shelf and reallocated to a new position. Our sales company were very good at doing relays and was often able to reposition the jams in a more advantageous spot.

With the help of Twin Agencies, our share of the jam market grew, and so did Wayne's business. As our share in the supermarkets grew, so did their demands.

We were, pressured into preparing and setting dates for the year's specials with a minimum of four. If a deal was made with one chain of supermarkets, the opposition pressed for the same deal or better. The products were specialled in progressive stores one week and opposition the following week. The supermarkets kept a wary eye on suppliers to make sure they got the same deal or better, and it did not pay to upset them!

We did no other advertising, only specials and end displays in the supermarkets, and we achieved the ninth largest growth in the shelf stable edible category, going from forty-fifth to thirtieth in the category rankings.

Owen knew from his experience how much of a challenge launching a new grocery product was, but he was always quick to praise the supermarket chains for their support. He understood and worked with the knowledge that establishing relationships with buyers, agents, and carriers took time.

Our lack of paid advertising was commented upon in the December 2001 *Marketing Magazine.* Our growth with no promotional spend was based on the old-fashioned concept of a great product that consumers really liked. Packaging and promotion might encourage people to buy a product, but if the experience doesn't live up to the promise, they won't buy it again. The main reason for our growth is that people try our products in restaurants or at a friend's house, and then they go on to buy it themselves and become loyal customers.

Owen and I felt truly blessed because our sales kept growing and growing!

The Blackcurrant Saga

Our son Tim brought energy and a vision to expand the product range when he joined the business and decided to add a blackberry jam. After our factory manager trialled the three main fruit varieties of blackberries grown in New Zealand, Ben Ard, Ben Rua, and Magnus (a very flavoursome jam using Magnus blackcurrants), finally passed Owen's taste test. With its more intense acid flavour, Magnus made the best jam. Blackcurrant jam was quickly accepted by the supermarkets and became popular with the many New Zealanders who remembered tailing blackcurrants picked from their home gardens, and of course their health benefits had been well publicised in a marketing campaign by the Blackcurrant Co-operative.

Sourcing the blackcurrants was no easy task. At first they were purchased from the producer board at one dollar per kilogram. However, the following year when we entered the Chamber of Commerce Business Awards, the chairman of the Blackcurrant Co-operative was one of the judges. Our entry included detailed financial accounts and the profit margin on our blackcurrant jam. The following season, the price of blackcurrants jumped from one dollar to two dollars thirty cents per kilogram with no explanation, although I am sure a world price increase is a good reason.

The blackcurrant situation five years later resulted in a glut of currants on the market, maybe a direct result of setting too high a price and enabling others into the market. Owen would say it is more practical to wind yourself up, increase production, keep the price down, and not tempt others into the market for a quick and easy return. The price increase forced us to look elsewhere for our blackcurrants. Therefore we moved our purchase of blackcurrants from the co-operative to a local grower and purchased the yearly requirements at a price that was satisfactory to him and us. Because the fruit grown in our area was sent to Canterbury to be put through the destrigging machine to take the tails off, we had to come up with a method to do this ourselves. Our enterprising team on the farm invented their own destrigger with Owen's help. It was a mesh cylinder driven with a motor, which turned like a concrete mixer. Small quantities of frozen blackcurrants were tipped into the rotating cylinder, where the tails fell through the mesh, leaving a reasonably tail-free fruit.

Then the Blackcurrant Co-operative decided to hold a meeting to inform growers and manufacturers that they were changing the varieties of berries they wanted farmers to grow in the future. Owen sent our production manager to attend the meeting, but not before warning him about what to expect. 'The farmers will *not* be looking to produce crops in response to our needs as manufacturers. They will be growing a crop which requires as little work as possible for the greatest production and the greatest return. Ben Ard will be the berry of choice because it's easy growing, high producing, and resistant to pests and disease.'

It surprised our manager to learn that what Owen had predicted happened at the meeting. The farmers wanted to grow the varieties of fruit that they found easiest to grow, even though it may not be a variety of the manufacturers' choice.

The manager of the Blackcurrant Co-operative stated at the meeting that they were already growing limited production of the fruit manufacturers preferred, which was Magnus, as well as a few more of the variety that the manufacturers would reluctantly take (Ben Rua), and they were planting more of the variety manufacturers didn't want, the Ben Ard. The price fell dramatically in the 2004 blackcurrant season and resulted in many farmers being forced to sell up. On reflection, was it the varieties that caused the problem, the price, or cheap imports? How desirous are farmers to co-operate with manufacturers?

As the next chapter will show, farmers are stubborn – and they have clout!

The Calicivirus

In 1995 Australia and New Zealand began a jointly funded project to investigate the feasibility of using a strain of the RCD virus as a biological control agent for rabbits. Trials were undertaken at the Australian Commonwealth Scientific and Industrial Research Organisations' high-security Animal Health Laboratory in Geelong, Victoria, followed by field trials on Wardang Island, five kilometres off the South Australian coast. However, in October 1995 the RCD virus escaped from the island and became established, on the Australian mainland. A vaccine for the virus was registered, and the Australian government decided to regulate, for the release of the virus.

A year later, New Zealand farmers saw it as a solution, to their economic woes caused by rabbits in their area decimating pasturelands and crops, especially in Central Otago. I was told by a local that here in the rolling hills, rabbits were so dense they were mistaken for a hill – until they got up and ran away. Whether true or not, it was an impressive way of defining their problem!

In June 1996, the RCD Applicant Group, comprising a number of South Island Regional Councils and one North Island Council; Federated Farmers; and the Commissioner of Crown Lands lodged an application to import RCD virus into New Zealand.

This was happening while Owen and I were living in Auckland, doing our supermarket promotional visits from March to April 1997. In Auckland people were queuing up outside the supermarkets we visited in order to sign one of the many petitions circulated against the release of the disease. The country was divided on the issue. Animal lovers were very much against its release, but farmers from the South Island were lobbying, and making applications to the government to import it. Twelve months later, the deputy director-general of agriculture received 856 submissions against importation, along with several petitions. Being concerned about liability, he declined the application. Then in the spring of 1997, on the verge of the rabbit birthing season, highland farmers began importing from Australia the internal organs of rabbits who had died of calicivirus. They pureed the organs in blenders with bait such as oats, jam, or carrots, and they spread the mixture around rabbit warrens.

At the time that the virus was being released in this unorthodox manner, Owen and I were travelling to a Vineyard conference in Queenstown. As we approached the township, we were met by a police roadblock to find that cars were being searched for the virus in the hopes of containing it. But it was too late. The news was out, and farmers admitted that the RCD virus was being used. By August the virus was so widespread that eradication and containment were no longer a feasible option.

The farmers' actions were reported on and made headlines in the *Dominion* (19/9/1997) – 'A bio-security failure', the government called it. We called it an embarrassment!

As the news broke about the release of the virus, our plastic jam pot got some unwelcomed attention! Paul Holmes, a New Zealand broadcaster on his Television One tonight show, held up our Anathoth raspberry jam pot with the label pointed right into the camera, saying, 'An ideal container for another product: a blender mix of rabbit organs containing calicivirus – a rabbit smoothie!'

After this news item showing the calicivirus in our jam pots, our sales agent, Twin Agencies, implored us to make a statement, condemning its use. Owen didn't know how to respond, so he did nothing! We had a very strong customer base in the South Island who favoured the release, and on the other side of the argument was our developing North Island market, where the customers were against release. Caught between a rock and a hard place, the wisest option seemed to be to do nothing. Even when the hullaballoo died down, people still remembered our jam pot containing the virus. Fortunately for us, it had no effect on our jam sales, although the 'humour' of the situation continued to haunt us. In 2003, when we came through customs at the Auckland Airport after a meeting with Woolworths in Sydney, a young man in attendance for the agriculture and fisheries read the information on our entry card, and he asked what business we were into. On discovering it was jam, he quickly responded, 'Ah-ha, the pots with the calicivirus!'

Genealogy

The past is a great starting point with many lessons for the future. Owen's quest to find out more about his family led him to the Internet. He employed John Bullock, from a Nelson Media business, to help build a software programme to record his family tree. His website, Owenpope.com, has become a multimedia site designed to inspire, entertain, and hopefully add to the collective knowledge of the Pope family. The site provides links between family members and contains photos and profiles of members of the Pope family. In July 2001 the first sections of the website went live. Owen has always been interested in why people react in certain ways, why certain traits are passed on from one generation to the other, and why (if we really understood the past) we have to keep reinventing the wheel. He sought to do something about it by starting with the idea of building the Pope family tree, and through this he became riveted by a story that spans from the sixteenth century till today. His ancestors, who up until now were just figures that existed, started to take on real personalities, and his curiosity burgeoned even more. Realising that some of these ancestors were in fact still alive and had direct knowledge of the early twentieth century inspired him to undertake travel to meet them.

These meetings in New Zealand and around the world have produced a wealth of contacts and launch points for his research. His early belief that families pass on unique connections was confirmed when we travelled to England in 2000 and again in 2001. Here he witnessed first-hand similar mannerisms noted as peculiar to one cousin in New Zealand appearing in another cousin in Britain or Australia. These people had never met or known of each other's existence. Owen had always believed the Popes were and are a thoroughly enterprising lot, probably more by intuition than fact. Then he discovered Richard and John Pope and their inextricable links to the British Coal Mining Industry in the mid-1800s. These two men were leaders in the industry and, because of this position, were responsible for the development of mining techniques and transportation networks.

It has been through this ongoing project of studying his family history that Owen became convinced that it helps us to better understand ourselves as families and individuals, as well as giving us identity. Owen is the sort of person who is always busy with the present and the future, so naturally he believes that a quarter of a century beyond this point will be immensely exciting. 'Communication with people will be on a completely different basis than at the moment. It will be more interactive in ways that we can only imagine. We won't be separated by distance or time, and it will be this that will make the biggest contrast between the future and today. We will be able to communicate with anyone anywhere,' he says.

Owen hopes that when the family looks at this website, they will see and experience a strong message of value in education, enterprise, and maintaining good relationships with people. If this is the message they take from today to the future, then his job will have been done well.

Compliance Programmes

How could we ensure that the jams and pickles that we were producing were safe for customers to eat? In the start-up of our business, we relied on Owen's and my experiences and skills. But as our jam manufacturing grew and we moved further away from oversighting the day-to-day operation, we needed to ensure that our jams and pickles retained their quality and that the factories retained their efficiency.

Initially Owen had replaced himself with a food scientist, in order to develop and oversee the production in our first factory. Then with the increase in production, he augmented that number to four. Because food technologists study the physical, chemical, and biological properties of food, their knowledge and intellect was needed in our absence to oversee and maintain the manufacturing processes of our products and keep their taste and nutritional value.

A compliance programme tailored to meet the needs of our business was also essential to ensure contamination free products. Compliance with regulatory requirements, along with our own policies, were critical components of effective risk management to support our objectives. Therefore, Owen and I engaged an outside consultant to assist us in writing a hazard analysis and critical control point programme for our food-processing factories. It took us many hours of work over a twelve-month period and thirty thousand dollars to complete!

Time for a New Factory

With our production of raspberry jam, the internal room in our shed had outgrown its capacity. We had three factory employees and a manager, who was a qualified food technician, working in a very confined space. We were still hand filling and lidding, but our ambition to mechanize the filling could not be realized in our existing facility.

At this stage in the business, Owen had done the exercise of costing the offsite freezing that we were using, and with the tonnage of raspberries now being produced, it had become cost effective to build our own freezer on the farm. Therefore a factory with a storeroom alongside and a freezer unit behind became our goal.

By mid-1999, we were ready to build our new factory and freezer in time for the next raspberry season. Owen designed the factory with a double row of twelve burners in the centre back to back, giving us the capacity to produce a ton of raspberry jam a day. One staff member was allocated to each side of the twelve burners. A filling station was set up down one end, with a mechanical filling machine. The jam was emptied into a hopper and pumped up into the newly purchased filling and lidding machine. Once it had filled the jam pot, the machine pressed on the lid and flipped it out of the carousel upside down. The person on the filling station checked each pot and placed it into cartons ready for storage. With our new factory and four other offsite factories, we had expanded our manufacturing capacity to meet new markets.

Peta Mathias Came to Our House

Peta Mathias, a prolific chef, author, broadcaster, and television presenter, became interested in our jams and contacted Owen to ask how we operated. When he told her we harvested our raspberries, froze them down, and processed them into jam, she got excited and wanted to film the whole operation, for her upcoming programme called *Taste New Zealand*. Owen knowing that our new factory and freezer was expected to be operating by the following raspberry season, suggested that the best time to visit would be in December, when we were harvesting our raspberries.

When the day arrived for the visit, we were so excited. I was instantly captivated by her vibrant personality and her charming and witty conversation. She was able to put us at ease right away. It was a privilege to observe her hard at work, memorizing scripts and redoing scenes until the filming was perfected – an unforgettable day! I remember her saying that when envious people asked how she got such a good job, she would reply, 'Twenty years of bloody hard work!'

Although filming took place in December, it was not broadcast on television until late July 2000, when Owen and I were in England researching our family tree. Our son Tim was managing the business in our absence. We received a desperate phone call for help, begging us to come home. After the programme went to air, our jam sales went from 9 per cent of the market to 18 per cent! The programme continued to rerun over the next few months and was played on the Cook Strait Ferry during the summer, which increased our sales even more.

Then just three years later, in 2003, we were lucky to have Peta Mathias visit us again when she introduced our new products to her viewers: lemon marmalade, fruit salad jam, and beetroot chutney. The media write-ups again were very complimentary, and *The Grocer's Review* wrote that our products were some of the most outstanding jams, marmalades, chutneys, pickles, and relishes in the country. It also said that the marmalade had a terrific balance of sweetness and tartness – just right with a serious marmalade taste without tipping over into being too bitter. The fruit salad jam was sweet with a pleasant and subtle combination of fruit flavours. But it was the sweet and well-balanced beetroot chutney that got the enthusiastic response and approval from all who tried it, including the Cordon Bleu–qualified chef.

This positive media attention was the envy of all jam and pickle manufacturers as our sales continued to grow. Not even our difficult-to-pronounce brand name or our basic plastic packaging slowed us down.

Pickles and Chutneys Added

While our apricot grower was manufacturing apricot jam, yeast got into his product, and it began to ferment. He put the jam in the freezer to slow down the fermentation. We tried reheating the jam to kill the yeast but discovered that reheating affected the colour, making it darker. Dark apricot jam loses its appeal to customers because the colour denotes freshness in customers' minds.

In reaching out for a solution to the problem, I happened to be lucky enough to find a recipe for turning jams into pickles. I found the recipe in an ancient Otago University recipe book, which resourceful women apparently used after World War Two. By turning the apricot jam into apricot chutney, we were able to give the farmer a return for the product, which covered his manufacturing costs. Then we found our customers enjoyed the recycled apricot chutney so much that we had to modify the recipe and continue production using fruit instead of the jam! As with any product we developed, the supermarkets were quick to accept the apricot chutney, and it sat alone on the pickle section of the supermarket, for quite some time before other new pickle and chutney lines joined it.

We had not planned it, but the pickle line was set to continue simply out of opportunity. It happened when we met a young man from Waimate who grew zucchinis. He told us that his mum made the most delicious zucchini pickle.

After he gave us a pot of zucchini pickle, Owen could not keep his spoon out of it, and because he prides himself on having an average palate, he knew this product would be a winner. All we had to do was convince the zucchini grower to make the product for us to sell, which they did for six months or more – and then as production went up, they gave up! We were still at the trial stage by selling only at the Nelson market, but because customer demand was there, we could see that production needed to continue.

We found a zucchini grower in our district, and Owen tried to persuade him to process and freeze his zucchinis to make the pickle, but like many farmers he was not interested. However, he came to an arrangement whereby he would sell us his zucchini for a reasonable price, when the price on the market was so low that they were not worth picking. It was a good arrangement for both parties, although it was not always easy to respond to the grower-dictated times. Corporate entities could not facilitate an agreement such as this, but Owen was sympathetic to his plight, and we walked out our values by cooperating with farmers in order to get them a decent return for their crops.

In 2002 Owen read a report in the newspaper that accused zucchinis of causing a health problem to consumers. We had frozen down zucchinis for pickle, and so he needed to find out more. Fortunately an article in *Butterflies and Wheels* ('Green Myth vs. the Green', 5 February 2004, by

Thomas R. DeGregori) clarified the issue for us, and we lost none of our stock.

When the zucchini is attacked by insects, apparently they generate their own toxic insecticide to protect themselves. Owen was relieved it only occurred, with organically grown zucchinis that hadn't been protected with an insecticide. It is ironic that healthy, organically grown vegetables are capable of manufacturing toxic substances that are harmful to humans.

Following the success of our zucchini pickle, Tim was keen to add a spicy vegetable pickle to the line, so he got together with his father, and they came up with a recipe for a product they named Farmstyle. When added to the line, it turned out to be a better seller than the zucchini. Once again, in cooperation with the farmer, the cauliflowers were purchased when the market price was so low the farmer would be forced to plough them under. After a single phone call to us, they could recoup production costs. Owen worked hard in our relationships with growers to accommodate the market price swings on their crops, and we were always able to give them a reasonable return.

Not long after that, the Mahana factory saw an opportunity to increase production by manufacturing tomato relish. After consultation and many trials with Owen, a recipe was decided upon, and production commenced. Then Owen followed up with a year of trials in 2003 and added a beetroot chutney that replicated the longed-for sweet flavour of our mother's preserved beetroot.

Some reviews from food writers suggested that there was no point in making one's own jams and pickles, because Anathoth preserves were readily available in all supermarkets!

An Apricot Shortage

In December 2000 our apricot grower visited and told us that because of a nationwide crop failure, all his apricots were going into export and local market. The shortage on the local market meant excellent returns for his fresh apricots, and he would then be unable to supply apricot jam.

I remembered that years before, when the price of raspberries went up, we had been in the same position and were forced to choose between the high price offered or continuing to make jam. Although the high price for our fruit that year was tempting, we had chosen to continue with the jam. The market return for fruit was volatile, prices were up and down, and in the past we'd had no control on our income. Better the dollar you can earn than rely on the dollar you might, I always thought. The jam is a reliable business guaranteeing a reasonable return. Unlike our apricot grower, we were building a business for the long haul and had made a deliberate choice over a one-time return.

Owen felt let down with the apricot shortfall and was concerned for the reputation of our business. Continuity of supply was of the utmost importance to the supermarkets, and his reputation with them was in jeopardy. He was now obliged to source apricots for the next year's production or take the jam off the shelf, as our grower had suggested.

But as a man of action, he took control of the situation by travelling south to Roxburgh, in Central Otago, where the best apricots were grown. He purchased 120 tons of apricots for processing at a $1.25 a kilogram, and even at $1.50, which he and the farmers considered, a fair price for processing fruit picked straight from the tree and put into a bin.

Farmers were and still are lucky to get eighty cents a kilogram, and sometimes even a lower price than this, from other manufacturers. When Owen was buying produce, he would always calculate the price of growing the crop and then generously add the farmer's living cost to it to ensure that his suppliers were still able to supply in years to come. I do not know, nor have I heard of, any other manufacturers who work this way. Farmers are sometimes driven out of the industry if manufacturers don't pay a reasonable price for raw materials. Manufacturers prefer to import cheaper raw materials, stating a shortage in crops such as apricots and raspberries as an excuse, than give local growers a decent return.

In his forward planning for the business, Owen had anticipated that raspberries of good variety and quality were not easy to come by, so he was leasing land from a neighbour and planting more. Now because of seasonal fluctuations, apricots were also going to be in short supply, and he was compelled to ensure ongoing supplies for the jam. Apricot growers in Roxburgh were pushed out of the industry with threats of imports forcing low returns, and that meant Owen needed to ensure our supplies by investing in orchards. It was during his visit to Roxburgh that he had the opportunity to purchase two apricot orchards at what he considered a very reasonable price, with the owners prepared to stay on and manage them. After Owen had purchased apricots, unbeknownst to him, his apricot grower had reconsidered and purchased apricots, so we now had an oversupply of apricots. What a predicament!

With enough apricots for two years of jam production, Tim came up with a new recipe for fruit salad jam using apricots, pineapple, and passion fruit, which was readily accepted by the supermarkets. Customers loved putting it on top of their Pavlovas.

Later that year, our apricot grower changed the direction of his business. We purchased his manufacturing, but losing the production capacity from the apricot factory meant that we had to expand our operation in the Moutere by building two new factories and a larger cool store.

New Factories and Cool Store

Despite the benefits that came from other farmers investing in our business, that plan also came with risks and challenges. When placing manufacturing activities in the hands of a manufacturing partner, we ensured we retained control and managed tasks through documented business processes and contractual agreements. But when the apricot grower suddenly exited the manufacturing, and we needed to run our factory on twenty-four-hour shifts, the capital expenditure of new factories seemed to be justifiable and necessary to support the continuing supply of products. Although factories built on farms where the produce was grown is an ideal situation, at this stage of our business, it had become financially advantageous and necessary to hold on to the manufacturing. Already a new storeroom to hold all the incoming stock from suppliers was planned, and the Bank of New Zealand agreed: why not new factories?

Our two new factories and freezer were built and ready for use by January 2002. Our $500.000 factory consisted of two separate, identical factories with large cooking areas. They had a long, stainless steel bench into which individual wok-type gas rings were set on either side. The jam pans were placed into the woks for cooking. The new building included a huge freezer unit capable of storing four to five hundred tons of fruit and vegetables.

Official Opening

A special ceremony was held in February 2002 for the opening of the new factories and freezer. Jim Anderton, Deputy Prime Minister and Minister for Industry, Regional, and Economic Development, officially opened the new building. He applauded our innovation, saying that it was a privilege to be associated with such innovative people, and he added if the country wanted more jobs and rising incomes for the entire nation, New Zealand needed to repeat the success of Anathoth in hundreds of companies up and down New Zealand.

Damien O'Connor, MP for West Coast/Tasman, was also there, along with a special guest, cereal magnate Dick Hubbard, who had stayed overnight with us. Dick also spoke and said we underpinned a remarkable story about what hard work could achieve. Not only did we share the same marketing company with Dick, but we also shared the same business ideals and values.

Nick Smith, National Party Member of Parliament for Nelson, told us that Anathoth products are international ambassadors for Nelson's sunshine and horticultural industries, and it has become the taste equivalent of Nelson's Wearable Arts. Both started from humble beginnings but have exploded into major enterprises of which every Nelsonian was proud.

Our business was a family business using locally grown produce with a different and more individual approach to production, in order to give better quality control. Growers were adding value to their crops and making bigger margins – an operator scheme that brought handsome rewards.

It was truly a memorable day to have the deputy prime minister, the cereal king Dick Hubbard, and all our staff present for the opening of our new facilities, which were built to allow us to serve our growing Australasian market.

Owen explains to the deputy prime minister how the factory operates.

Although Coles and Woolworths were ready to take our products, Owen was cautious as always, knowing that the potential for further sales was huge. He eased into Australia gradually, making sure all orders could be filled. State by state was what Coles had promised!

Export Preparation

Owen's vision for the Australian market and his contacts within were growing, and he was hungry to open new markets across the Tasman. Our expatriate New Zealanders were taking jam back to Australia, and customers developed an insatiable appetite for it. It was time to learn about exporting! A few years earlier, Owen had wanted to know how the regulations and systems worked, and how much time and cost were involved, when exporting stock into Australia. He had used a hands-on approach. Under the free trade agreement with Australia, no license or permit was required, so the paperwork was easy. Then it was a matter of flying a few boxes of jam to Melbourne. A taste of the Australian's system was then experienced when the jam arrived. Owen was notified that it was in quarantine and was ready to be collected.

Upon reaching the airport quarantine station, we were told that we needed release documents from customs. We walked the short distance to the customs office and joined the long queue, waiting patiently until one of the employees from the six windows called us up. After identifying himself, Owen requested his documentation.

'I cannot let this jam into the country. It is not allowed,' the clerk officiously responded.

Owen politely pointed out that it was possible to bring jam in under the free trade agreement Australia had with New Zealand.

'There's the manual over there, find it, then, if it's there!' the haughty reply came back as he pointed to a shelf behind us on the back wall of the office.

Owen knew that all procedures in government are controlled by regulations, so he confidently strolled to the shelf and found the enormous manual. To my astonishment, he quickly turned to the regulations covering jam imports. He filled out the form with the relevant section numbers quoted and then returned to the clerk at the counter, who looked at him in surprise and astonishment at his speedy return. After a short confab with two of his comrades, he finally had to agree that the regulations permitted entry. With a disgruntled thump, he stamped the release documents. Owen paid the fees, collected the jam, and established the procedures that needed to be followed by our office staff to bring jam into Australia.

By doing, this exercise Owen had saved a fair amount of dollars that perhaps other companies would have to spend on an import clerk, and he was now more knowledgeable about the difficulties that might be encountered during export.

It took major companies several years to discover that relevant clause in the regulations covering jam imports from New Zealand, and it is one of the reasons why all Australian jams are now manufactured in New Zealand.

A Call from Australia

By 2002 the extensive test marketing into Australia had recorded positive sales growth at Ritchie supermarkets in Melbourne, Victoria. The demand for our product was growing and had become a standout success. There had been a long developmental process in balancing the goal of batch-making three kilograms at a time, maintaining a high-quality, consistent product and the need to produce the quantities for export into a country as large as Australia. We were expecting significant growth over the next few years, and it was an exciting time to be involved in the business. Coles and Woolworths were ready and waiting! They were monitoring our sales in the Ritchie stores, and we had been getting a very positive response from buyers when we visited their head offices. Regular visits were made to the Melbourne stores, and Tim spent much of his time researching the two hundred Australian spreads market, convinced, that we had a fighting chance at breaking through a saturated market. There were fifteen to twenty other brands all competing on price and quality, but no one was making a jam quite like ours, and we were confident the demand from ex-patriots was mounting.

Now with the opening of the new factory and cool store manufacturing, capacity was at a level high enough to make exporting container-loads of jam to Australia a reality. On the back of financial help and advice from Geoff Dangerfield of Industry New Zealand, our apricot orchards in production, 130 tons of raspberries from the Upper Moutere orchard, and other supply contracts with growers in place, we were ready and confident about meeting orders.

Owen was focused on building relationships with the buyers of both Woolworths and Coles, and he did not lose touch with what was going on with their new products programme. Then came the phone call from Neil Worrall, the buyer from the Coles head office in Melbourne. Owen and I had been visiting Woolworths and Coles head offices for four years before we got this long-awaited phone call.

'We are looking for a new jam for our supermarkets. I want to see you in our office Monday morning,' Neil said.

On that Monday morning meeting towards the end of 2002, Neil laid out the plan to put our jam into the supermarkets state by state. It was expected to take six months in the lead-up to the launch, so he wanted to see our man over there every month starting January, until the launch date. Owen replied that he was quite prepared to do whatever it took to get the job done. We left the meeting excited that the years of preparation were coming to fruition, and we would be in the Australian Coles chain of supermarkets in six months' time, by mid-2003.

Owen geared the business up by employing more staff in preparation for the expansion. We were anticipating the Australian market to be six times the size of New Zealand,

and so the structure needed to be in place to handle the expected increase in sales.

After the first month's appointment date had passed, Owen phoned our sales agent to ask him how the meeting with Neil went. He replied that he hadn't gone to the meeting, but it was okay because he had set up an appointment for the following month. Before the next monthly meeting came around, our sales agent rang to say that Coles was not going to take the jam because they were putting another jam into the slot previously reserved for us. Owen was bitterly disappointed but understood exactly why Neil from Coles would do this. Our representative, for some unknown mysterious reason, had impaired our entry by not turning up for the first meeting. The buyer had been offended, and it had given him no confidence in our business. Our years of preparation for this big event had just been sabotaged. The disappointment was huge!

The monthly magazine for the food and drink industry, *FMCG,* reported in their April issue that the IXL brand entered Coles in plastic pots, obviously taking our place. They had launched a range of preserves in polypropylene jars with enclosable lids in typical Australian fashion, saying, 'Thank you for the idea, Anathoth!'

The IXL brand had taken our spot by trying to market their jam in a plastic pot. However, the product in the plastic pot was of such poor quality that sales did not eventuate.

Our successful sales at the Ritchie stores soon proved too much for the big guys to overlook, so later in the year, Coles and Woolworths again made a spot available, opening the door for negotiations with us for entry into their supermarkets.

In December 2003 the buyer from the Woolworths head office in Sydney called us in. It cost us an arm and a leg to get our team over there on short notice. The team included Tim, Owen, me, and our sales representative. During this visit, the female buyer gave us instructions on how to prepare for entry into their stores.

After our export sales agent and his marketing company had let us down by manipulating the situation, Owen decided he would include himself in negotiations and the leg work within the Australian market.

Mark, Shelley, Tim, Kaye and Owen in the storeroom with pallets of jam ready for export.

A Sound Business Legacy

By 2003 Owen had a history of sound financial management. The growth of our business was the envy of many, and our equity was growing year by year. We were well poised and ready to explode into the export market and eventually fulfil Owen's vision of taking Anathoth to the world.

Our financial records for the last three years showed growth.

Year	Turnover	Profit	Assets	Equity	%
2001	$6,520,452	$118,360	$2,946,560	$561,905	19.07%
2002	$9,476,281	$261,793	$3,767,655	$1,014,772	26.93%
2003	$11,143,539	$762,932	$5,177,099	2,165,231	41.82%

Our number of employees had increased.

- 2001: 20 permanents, 315 casual hand-picking fruit
- 2002: 54 permanents, 503 casual hand-picking fruit
- 2003: 71 permanents, 190 casuals, plus 3 picking machines

We had a seven-computer network, a full-time accountant, an off-site consultant accountant, and an accounting firm to consult. Our administration team included a receptionist, marketing manager, and two factory managers employed to meet the Australian market, as well as a procurement manager and four farm managers, two for apricot orchards and two for the raspberry gardens. Each of our three farms had its own company name and operated as a separate entity in order to ensure the profitability of each and identify inefficiencies.

Monitoring stock quantities and reordering raw materials was done by the factory manager, the on-site office staff handled invoicing, and the sales team e-mailed pallet orders via the system. Every day, a bill of materials recorded each factory's production and was entered on the computer to update the final cost of each pot of jam or pickle.

The computer system was efficient and controlled expenditure. It did everything from entering invoices to receiving in stock. When stock came in, a purchase order was generated and matched with the creditor's invoice against the packing slip and entered into the accounts.

The only thing the system did not do was forecasting, and Owen was considering a software package called WinForecast for cash budgeting projections. The programme answered questions like whether it was actually good for the company to sell ten thousand pots more of raspberry jam this month, if stocks of fruit ran out and more need to be purchased.

He was working with a local accounting firm, West Yates, to see how cash flow would be affected by adjusting selling price and quantities sold.

Owen had also developed a company website, which at this time was primarily a marketing tool and was not used for online sales.

After having built up a strong brand with the potential growth of sales to make it a multi-million-dollar business in just fifteen years, it was little wonder that Ernst and Young invited Owen into the Entrepreneur of the Year competition in 2003!

Owen Pope – The Bloke

Owen awoke from his life as a shy country lad when he arrived at boarding school, which he found to be a comforting and welcoming place. He enjoyed the encouragement and the sense of purpose of belonging, and socializing with a group of his peers brought out his previously hidden gregarious nature. In the years following, he learnt to become a great storyteller and often captivated his audience with his true-life experiences. Throughout his working life, he enjoyed the many challenges that each job brought. Then after becoming a Christian in his forties, life took on a new meaning and purpose. When he heard the parable of the Talents from Matthew 25:14–30, he took this parable to be an encouragement to use his God-given gifts in God's service, and to take risks for the sake of the kingdom of God. He believed his failure to use his gifts, as the parable suggested, would result in severe judgement. After this discovery, he left the safety of government employment and stepped out to work for himself.

Owen enjoyed being his own boss and responded enthusiastically to working for himself. He loved taking his time over two or more morning cuppas, enjoying the time to prepare for the day's work. In the early days on the farm, he set up his Renoface business, cultivated the raspberry garden, and tended the sheep. He worked long hours, needed very little sleep, and devoted much of his waking hours to improving all aspects of his businesses. As our jam manufacturing grew and administration became a large part of the business, he never moved far from the kitchen table, where he brought all his business associates. Our home was an extension of our business and a place of hospitality for family, employees, and all who wanted to do business – and it was business twenty-four seven!

He offered solutions to any problem employees were having, be it childcare or sickness, and he was quick to observe a problem as he moved among his workers. He always appeared to be fighting fires, but there was no panic in him because he was always quietly confident about finding a solution. He moved with new ideas and created systems for efficiency devoid of anxiety. He found it as easy to rectify relationship as he did equipment, and throughout our ownership of the business, he kept a finger on the pulse in order to maintain a healthy growing business.

By 2003 Anathoth had now become Owen Pope's story of innovation and making it happen. In New Zealand Dick Hubbard was known as the king of breakfast cereal, just as Owen Pope was known as the king of jam, as Anathoth Company now claimed 20 per cent of the New Zealand jams, pickles, and marmalades market. He attributed his success to the fact that knowing the customer's needs, being known by the customers, earning their trust and confidence, and providing a good and consistent product and service were the most important elements in building a brand and continuing its success. Building trusting, lasting relationships with those involved in marketing products takes time, and Owen's personal involvement in such dealings always provided a satisfying exchange. He sees intuitively and uses logical and analytical thought based on reason to solve difficult problems. He is not persuaded by fashionable arguments, fads, or actions.

By the time sales people approached Owen to sell their steam boilers and other mechanized processes used by opposition jam makers, Owen had done the exercise in quality and efficiency. Just as it was more efficient and necessary to make the best metal alloy with one small pot at a time, so too it was with jam making. No other method can evaporate the liquid to create the intensity of flavour that one small pan can.

Owen also understood how hard it was for manufacturers to watch the evaporation going out from the pot and not want to capture it, when they saw it as lost dollars. Yet he was never tempted to compromise the quality of his product or his system of jam making for more dollars. He understood his customers, and with an average pallet, he claimed that if he liked it, so would most of the population. Because of our success, he came to believe that any product sold in the supermarket could be made in small batches and receive the same market success as our jams and pickles. In his view, when a successful brand changed its method of manufacture, it would not only lose customers but would leave a gap in the market for someone to produce something better!

Owen is a person who plans his goals step by step; he builds trust with honesty, and every move he makes is intentionally designed to build a foundation for the future, not just a temporary buzz.

At the height of our success, as we were heading towards 22 per cent market share, Owen reckoned somewhere in the office of Heinz Watties there must be alarm bells that went off when a competing jam manufacturer got close to overtaking their leading brand, because Heinz Watties began a large campaign of advertising for their jam products. Along with Bill Connolly's advertising that Craig's jam stayed on your toast and was not runny like some jams, they also advertised on national television a recipe for using Craig's three-berry jam. It aired on Wednesday, and by Friday, the supermarket shelves throughout the country were empty of our Anathoth three berry jam. Needless, to say Heinz Watties never broadcasted that add again.

Owen didn't copy trends, pander to what's popular, or look at what a competitor might be doing. He decided that if he reacted to what his competitor was doing, then they were running his business! He liked to run his own race by making an informed decision on what was right for *his* business. Without enough information, no decision was made. That was how he built a business, and perhaps it was why he was so successful and blessed in building the strong Anathoth brand.

Owen was an entrepreneur!

Entrepreneur of the Year

In 2003 Anathoth won a coveted Cuisine Magazine Matua Valley award for innovation and excellence. Owen's success was being noticed and recognized by some corporate entities.

He was invited by Carol Hirschfeld to enter the 2003 Ernst and Young Entrepreneur of the Year competition. It was the second time he had been into an award, because he only entered when invited. That way he was more likely to win! He became a semi-finalist in the 2003 Ernst and Young Entrepreneur of the Year Competition, and he had flattering write-ups printed about him in the media throughout the country, which was good for business – any publicity increased sales! Owen deserved all the accolade that followed, because it was his insight and quiet confidence that had geared up the business at each stage of development.

Our company was now looked upon as one of New Zealand's more highly regarded niche food production companies. It was customer demand that had the supermarkets calling to order. Our popular raspberry jam was the first of our range, but over time additional fruit varieties were added, along with our pickles and chutneys.

We had invested heavily in our two new facilities and now had enormous capacity for expansion, with five other factories around the country, each created to specialize in one or two lines for our customers, who preferred flavoursome taste to mass production.

Despite the success he had achieved, Owen's greatest desire was for Anathoth to remain true to its roots and traditions, which was not going to be easy when faced with worldly influences and persuasions. The Anathoth brand was more than just a traditional recipe. It was made in the traditional way and was characterized as an authentic, handmade, artisan product, made in small batches to identify and protect the unique natural tastes that were in danger of being lost when mass production was involved. Owen proved that machinery could never replace the skills of a person who had developed the skills of our factory workers.

The Anathoth brand had a meaningful point of difference and delivered on that difference. Our personal story came with the brand and helped us to connect with customers, and in turn connect customers to the products. Our simple packaging was effective in communicating our values and in prompting people's choice when they went to select from the supermarket shelf.

The Anathoth brand consistently delivered on quality, flavour, and the homemade taste! We were easy to reach and readily available to ensure customer satisfaction, one of our highest priorities. We were there to service customers, and any dissatisfaction with a product was an opportunity to communicate with them and earn their trust.

Trust in a product, once earned, induces great loyalty from your customers, which will last through many production and ownership changes. Having these points of difference gave our brand a much higher potential for growth than any other brand in this category, as much as 15 per cent annually.

Owen displayed exceptional expertise at setting up our brand, and he utilized all his years of experience in various occupations to do so, but the skill most needed was the ability to accurately analyse situations and make the vital decisions that grew our business.

Entrepreneurs create small businesses, and it is a recognized fact that small businesses are the backbone of any economy. Small businesses work and stand for what is best for their employees, their communities and for the country.

By 2003 Owen had established a prosperous, working, integrated farming, manufacturing, and marketing business in Upper Moutere, Nelson.

This photo of our farm in 2003 shows the driveway to the house to the left, with its swimming pool beyond and a double garage with offices to the right. The grounds were landscaped over the last five years, and the trees and shrubs are maturing.

The first factory is beside the double garage and close to the house. Five cabins, which have become offices, are set along the entrance road that leads down to the two new factories, large storeroom, and the farm. Part of the raspberry garden is seen stretching beyond the buildings.

Our farm, factory, administration and sales offices in 2004

PART 5

Unfamiliar Territory

Owen's birthday was always a reason to celebrate, and I decided Catherine Cove Wilderness Resort on Durville Island would be his birthday treat! A restaurant, accommodations, and isolation sounded like the ideal place to get away from our farm and the demands of the business.

In order to reach Catherine Cove, we drove two and a half hours, to the small seaside village of French Pass, on the eastern side of the Marlborough Sounds. From French Pass, we left the car and took the water taxi, which was the only access into Catherine Cove. As the water taxi pulled into the jetty, a young man collected our bags and escorted us to our waterside chalet. The bay was so peaceful and tranquil that I knew I was going to enjoy the rest and relaxation, with no cell phone coverage or interruptions to demand our attention. After settling in and enjoying an evening meal and a quiet drink in the restaurant, we returned to our chalet to soak up the peace and quiet of the bay with its great, empty, tranquil expanse of water stretched out before us.

We were woken at daybreak by a chorus of native birds, and we found that our privacy had been invaded. Three vessels were now anchored in the once-empty bay: a yacht and a couple of launches. After breakfast in our chalet, we took an early morning stroll across the rocks, exploring the nooks and crannies of sea life and enjoying the sea air. After that, we were refreshed and ready to return to the cafe for a mid-morning cuppa.

While seated in the cafe, we heard a call come over the radio from the yacht in the bay, notifying the chef that they were coming in for lunch. Then as the morning progressed, groups of people began leaving their boats in the cove to come ashore, and the island became a hive of activity The restaurant turned out to be the meeting place for locals and boaties who either resided here permanently or had weekend residences or boats in the bay. And why not? They had a beautiful wilderness to enjoy, company when desired, and a restaurant with excellent service from a chef who was very obliging and able to present superb cuisine of choice.

To our surprise, the Wilkins from Motueka were amongst the group from the boat, so they joined us for dinner. The Wilkins family had planted their first apple trees the year we'd purchased our Upper Moutere farm, and now they were successful apple growers with fourteen orchards. It was inevitable that the conversation would turn to a discussion about business, problems, and solutions – and of course, our upcoming entry into Coles and Woolworths, Australia.

After a restful weekend on Durville Island, the year continued to be a busy one. Owen geared the business up to meet our export market. There was no way of knowing at this time that our contact with the Wilkes family would bring to light an investor who, like Owen, was an entrepreneur and was interested in the growing success of our Anathoth brand!

Raising Capital for Australia

When the Bank of New Zealand examined the growth and potential for our business across the Tasman, they suggested that we fund export growth with investors. Shortly after that suggestion, an opportunity for such investment arrived. It was in April 2003 that a real estate agent called at our home and asked if we were interested in selling our business, because he had a client who was interested in buying. Owen's immediate response was no, because we were about to export into Australia.

The agent then asked if there was an opportunity for financial investment. Our financial performance had been well documented for the Bank of New Zealand in our business plan. The bank had suggested that outside investors could fund our export market, so Owen needed to consider this proposition. He weighed the fact that an opportunity to inject more capital into the business while exporting into Australia was worth considering. The land agent informed Owen that his client wanted to explore the possibility of buying in, and he had enormous capital. Owen always wanted to be part of Anathoth, but he was interested in investment to assist the expansion. Investment at this stage was very tempting! It would put fewer constraints on growth and allow it to flourish. He agreed to meet with the investor's financial adviser, Ray Parker.

We were informed that Ray Parker was acting for Howard Paterson a Dunedin property developer worth about seventy-five million dollars. Howard was struggling to enter the supermarket with A2 milk and free-range eggs, and he saw the Anathoth products as a good fit to give him advantage with the supermarkets. After previewing our financial accounts for 2002–2004, Ray communicated that Howard Patterson was interested in moving forward.

Owen's humorous response in a return e-mail was, 'I am interested in moving forward and developing the business. If I wasn't, a phone call to Heinz Watties would probably return a high dividend just to remove the nuisance.'

Negotiations began. By spending a great deal of time visiting our farm and hours on the telephone examining Owen to find out what motivated him, Ray Parker was able to gain useful personal information to use in future negotiations. Owen said he got RSI from holding the telephone for long conversations, and he made a joke about the length of time Ray could talk. The family thought Owen had met his equal!

Ray gained Owen's confidence. He convinced Owen that Howard's intention was to grow the business by developing farms and manufacturing the products produced on those farms, with the same homemade system already practiced in our factories. What Howard had to offer was a governing board with financial expertise to support Owen in the expansion and growth of Anathoth to the Australian market. Shared responsibility, with financial experts like a maintenance crew, had a great deal of appeal for Owen.

The new company with joint ownership was to have leases on our farms and would continue supplying the fruit for jam making. With the expansion of the jam market into Australia, we would be short of raspberries, so in order to ensure continuity of fruit supply, Owen was to purchase farms recommended by the investors: a raspberry garden in Tapawera, and an apple orchard in Roxburgh, which the new company would plant out in other fruits for jam manufacture.

Ray Parker generously assisted Owen by preparing statements for bank loans, guiding him through all the paperwork in negotiating a share of our business. To purchase the new farms, it was necessary for us to borrow a significant amount of money, and Ray Parker again prepared the accounts with appropriate documentation ready to present the application to the bank. He also suggested that we had sufficient equity to have a million-dollar overdraft facility available that could be used to purchase other businesses to add to Anathoth in the future. The money paid for shares in the business would be available to buy the farms. Owen liked the plan and the prospect of working alongside the team of experts that Howard offered. He reckoned it looked like a great setup for the future growth of the Anathoth brand: expertise and money!

Due Diligence and a New Partner

Ray was a qualified chartered accountant and a former CEO of Tasman Agriculture. He was employed by Fonterra Co-op Group as GM of shareholder services.

In 2002 he developed his own business, specialising in private investment and management consultancy work, and in this capacity he acted for Howard Paterson. By the end of June, he had carried out due diligence on our business, as well as the evaluation of costs, benefits, and risks for the planned investment. Ray had employed Mary Watson, an investment analysis from Wellington, to assist him. According to Ray, Mary Watson had a very good technical and practical mind when it came to analysing businesses. At Ray's request, Mary had drawn up a thorough profile of what our business would look like in five years' time. While Owen and I were chatting informally with Mary, she told us that prior to coming to us, she had also done due diligence on Michael Barker, an opposition jam manufacturer, and it pleased us when she said, 'Your business is more profitable than Barker's.'

A price for the shares of our company were decided. It was to be three times the earnings before interest and tax (EBIT), which is a measure of a firm's profit that includes all expenses except interest and income tax expenses – the difference between operating revenues and operating expenses. There was no monetary value put on the brand, so the shares in Anathoth were only valued at two million eight hundred dollars.

Then legal documents from Ray Parker flew at Owen thick and fast, and there came a vast array of papers strewn across his desk. Our lawyer, Ian Duncan from Duncan and Cotterill, had recently moved from Dunedin to Nelson and protected our legal interests. He reassured Owen that this was a good deal because he knew Howard Paterson and gave him the thumbs-up and the 'very honest gentleman' label. The deal was coming together with verbal agreement all round, so a meeting with Howard in his Edinburgh Trust offices in Dunedin was set up for Friday, 29 June 2003, to make the final compatibility assessment.

'What do you think the Wilkins and I talked about over a glass of wine?' Howard said when we met him. 'I have always been interested in the growth of the business and the successful formula. In fact, this is the first business my wife has been keen to play a part in.'

These were Howard Patterson's words when we met him several weeks later. After spending some time with Howard on Friday, he flew off to Fiji, leaving Owen and me duly impressed with his enthusiasm for the upcoming union. Share Chat on 4 July 2003 confirmed that Howard Paterson was teaming up his eggs, venison, and milk with our Anathoth brand to facilitate entry into the supermarkets. Anathoth was a high-volume seller in the supermarkets, with 22 per cent of the market, and would provide powerful leverage with the supermarkets.

Mission Accomplished

After meeting with Howard in his office, Owen and I left feeling elated because the shared responsibility and oversight meant a new chapter in the expansion of our business was about to begin. Exciting times lay ahead for all of us. We had lived in our home for over eighteen years, brought up our kids, and looked after our parents. For me and my restless spirit, my heart had at last found a resting place – a major accomplishment!

Owen was confident his mission was being accomplished successfully. He always said if you don't expand, you die, and his passion for the success and growth of a farming-based business was strong. He was looking forward to embracing this new chapter in the story of Anathoth, knowing that the business he had birthed and nurtured into maturity was alive and well and set to continue with support from this day forward. He had acquired a unique dream, a burning desire to solve a farming problem. He had the courage to nurture it with a passion to make it grow beyond all expectations. From this viewpoint, his dream and mission had been completed successfully!

Integrated farming

Key Historical Milestones for the Growing, Manufacturing, and Marketing of Anathoth Jams and Pickles by Owen and Kaye Pope

1987 Owen and Kaye purchased a raspberry farm.

1989 Began selling raspberry jam at the Nelson Market.

1990 Applied to council to manufacture and retail jam. Converted garage into a small manufacturing facility.

1993 Advertised in the *Dairyman* and sold jam by mail order. Sold jam in the Christchurch Riccarton Rotary Market and Art Market on Saturdays and Sundays.

Entered the South Island supermarkets with raspberry jam. Began contract supply of sugar.

1994 Built accommodation for raspberry pickers.

1995	Blackberry grower built a facility and was trained to make jam, which was added to Anathoth range.
	Won Nelson Chamber of Commerce Small Business Award.
1996	Other jams introduced, and factories built on farms.
	Entered North Island supermarkets.
1998	Pickles and relishes introduced.
1999	Coverage on *Taste NZ* with Peta Mathias.
	New factory and cool store opened.
2001	Entered the Australian market.
2002	Opening of new factories and cool store on farm.
2003	Introduction of dressings.
	Owen nominated for Entrepreneur of the Year.
2003	August: Investors in the business.

Printed in the United States
By Bookmasters